ADVANCE PRAISE

From Auschwitz with Love is the story of the love between two sisters that emerged from a realm in which everything conspired against any such love. It is introspective and penetrating, taking the reader into the souls of the survivors of the Event and its aftermath, into the souls that were themselves the target of the Nazi evil. While the book's historical detail alone marks it as an invaluable contribution to Holocaust studies, its testimony to the dearness of human life threatened by the Holocaust makes it even more so. Indeed, with his elegance of style Daniel Seymour weaves a personal tale that transcends the history to take us into the depth dimension of the Shoah.

— David Patterson, Hillel A. Feinberg Professor of Holocaust Studies, University of Texas at Dallas.

From Auschwitz with Love is a fascinating book about the life stories of Manci and Ruth Grunberger. It is the story of the Holocaust, survival and rescue. At the same time, this is also the story of infinite love between two sisters. The love shapes who they become as individuals and gives them the strength to survive Auschwitz, cope with the rescue and temporary stay in Sweden, and with challenges of building new lives in the US. This well-written book is both captivating and insightful, and, as such, it is an important new contribution to Holocaust studies.

— **Roland Kostić, Associate Professor in Peace and Conflict Research Senior Lecturer in Holocaust and Genocide Studies, Uppsala University, Sweden.**

Manci and Ruth Grunberger's life story is fascinating, poignant, and convincing. It captivates the reader and historians will relish the details associated with their early lives in Mukacevo, Czechoslovakia. Their bond was unbreakable.

— **Kelly J. Zuniga, CEO, Holocaust Museum Houston.**

From Auschwitz with Love is a captivating and compelling account of the lives of two loving and devoted sisters ranging from their happy childhoods in eastern Europe to their terrifying Holocaust experiences that sought to systematically rob them of their humanity to the successful and fulfilling lives they built for themselves in the United States. The sisters' honest, moving and detailed first person memoirs, accompanied by helpful historical contextualization and illuminating photographs, are skilfully and insightfully interwoven to produce a praiseworthy work. Its account of victimization, human endurance and resilience, coping with trauma, deep and lasting friendships and sibling love should not be forgotten.

— **Elliot Lefkovitz, Adjunct Professor of Jewish History and Holocaust Studies, Spertus Institute for Jewish Learning and Leadership.**

From Auschwitz with Love is an intimate glimpse into the lives of two remarkable young women. Other than the *Diary of Anne Frank* which chronicles events as they happen, this book is unique from many other accounts as so much of this was captured in diary form by the two sisters just after they were liberated. Thus, many of the experiences they relay are fresh, vivid, and raw in their intensity. *From Auschwitz with Love* is an account that will live in history and a story that will never be forgotten. In capturing this story, Daniel Seymour has given the world a beautiful gift.

— **Nancy Sprowell Geise, author of *Auschwitz #34207 - The Joe Rubinstein Story*.**

From Auschwitz with Love is written with and for two sisters loving care by Daniel Seymour. Written in the first-person voice, the reader is transcended to their locale, witnessing the horrors of the Holocaust through their young eyes. Interwoven between the juxtaposing chapters is accurate historical information, so that the reader can put their experiences in context. What unfolds is an immersive read, and a real page-turner as the reader relives their hopes, dreams and fears.

— **Millie Jasper, Executive Director, Holocaust & Human Rights Education Center, White Plains, NY**.

This book offers a valuable and well-documented testimony. It portrays the struggles and achievements of two sisters who survived internment in the Auschwitz extermination camp. How could they summon the strength to start anew when their whole family was murdered? An essential emotional resource in their resilient process was their sisterly bond of love. Their gripping path demonstrates that human beings cannot be defined by the tragedy that fell upon them, but rather by how they responded to adversity. *From Auschwitz with Love* by Daniel Seymour is a skilfully woven narrative that sheds light on the coping mechanisms used by Manci and Ruthie to rebuild successful, yet dramatically contrasted lives.

— Françoise S. Ouzan, author of *How Young Holocaust Survivors Rebuilt Their Lives, France, The United States, and Israel*, Senior Research Associate, The Goldstein-Goren Diaspora Research Center, Tel Aviv University, Israel.

This inspiring memoir of two sisters' survival, devotion, success, and love is an authentic and an important contribution to giving women their voices. Daniel Seymour used their own words to write this book, which also includes his own short but scholarly background texts that give the sisters' testimony historical context. From Auschwitz with Love is, indeed, a love story between Manci and Ruth Grunberger.

— Rochelle Saidel, Founder and Executive Director, Remember the Women Institute and author of *The Jewish Women of Ravensbrück Concentration Camp*.

Daniel Seymour writes an eye-opening and painfully insightful book peering into the personal lives of Manci and Ruth Grunberger, two teenaged sisters, trapped in Hitler's death camps, who endured the horrors of the Holocaust and survived. This story will grip your heart, make you angry, and show you the true meaning of love. I highly recommend *From Auschwitz with Love*.

— **Denise George, co-author of *The Secret Holocaust Diaries*.**

This fast-paced narrative is driven by the memoirs and reflections of the women themselves, which were collected by author Daniel Seymour, who also introduces the book and provides historical background throughout. As the number of survivors decrease, *From Auschwitz with Love* reminds us anew of hope, dedication, loyalty and heroism of Ruthie and Manci and the other survivors. Their stories will continue to inspire us.

— **Paul Radensky, Senior Director for Education, Museum of Jewish Heritage - A Living Memorial to the Holocaust.**

As teenagers in Auschwitz, sisters Manci and Ruthie were forced to sort the personal belongings of newly arrived Jews while hearing the screams and pounding of walls from gas chambers nearby. Thanks to family encouragement, Manci's son-in-law Daniel Seymour took on writing their story. The result is a compilation of first-person interviews, memoir and diary entries with historical detail that provides a well-documented and poignant telling of two remarkable lives.

— **D.Z. Stone, journalist and author of *No Past Tense: Love and Survival in the Shadow of the Holocaust*.**

FROM AUSCHWITZ WITH LOVE

THE INSPIRING MEMOIR OF TWO SISTERS'
SURVIVAL, DEVOTION AND TRIUMPH AS TOLD
BY MANCI GRUNBERGER BERAN & RUTH
GRUNBERGER MERMELSTEIN

DANIEL SEYMOUR

ISBN 9789493231900 (ebook)

ISBN 9789493231887 (paperback)

ISBN 9789493231894 (hardcover)

Publisher: Amsterdam Publishers, The Netherlands

info@amsterdampublishers.com

Part of the series Holocaust Survivor Memoirs WWII

Readers' Favorite Silver Medal in the genre Non-fiction - Historical, 2022

Winner of the Feathered Quill Award 2023 in the memoir / biography category

Copyright © Daniel Seymour, 2022

Cover image: Family picture at Ancsi's Bar Mitzvah in 1937.

All Rights Reserved. No part of this publication may be reproduced or transmitted in any form or by any means, electronic or mechanical, including photocopy, recording or any other information storage and retrieval system, without prior permission in writing from the publisher.

CONTENTS

Foreword	xi
Introduction	xv
PART 1 Never Wanting	3
PART 2 Growing Storm	19
PART 3 Descent into Darkness	39
PART 4 On the Run	71
PART 5 Paradise	83
PART 6 The Philadelphia Story	101
PART 7 Lives Lived	115
The Kitchen Table	165
Epilogue	167
Sources	173
Acknowledgments	177
About the Author	179
Amsterdam Publishers Holocaust Library	180

FOREWORD

From Auschwitz with Love tells the story of two sisters, Manci and Ruthie, and the unfaltering family bond that allowed them to survive Auschwitz. It was, in the end, such unflagging devotion that saved them.

Manci and Ruthie were young girls when they were rounded up and sent to Auschwitz. Eight members of their immediate family also suffered the same fate, including a baby sister, culled and murdered by Nazis.

The two sisters have different personalities. Manci describes herself as more decisive, "a take charge kind of person." She loved school and even graduated from university after the war. Independent and spirited, Manci is neither religious nor close to Israel, instead she has focused on travelling and making the best of her life. She has always looked after Ruthie, three years her junior. Ruthie has always been more "accommodating" and "complacent." She likes to help out, look after children, and care for her home. Ruthie is religious and feels a kinship both to religious traditions and to Israel.

The two sisters have always been unconditionally devoted to each other. This sisterly bond was so powerful that it gave them the hope, courage, and strength to stay alive in Auschwitz.

The book begins with a description of the late period of World War II and of those ethnically diverse and tolerant Jews born in a faraway region (the sub-Carpathians). The Hungarians, the Nazis' zealous assistants, gradually imposed their own brutal antisemitic abuse and exactions, until that day in April 1944 when a so-called "private transport" rounded up a group of Jews and sent them to Auschwitz in horrific conditions. Daily existence in an extermination camp can sadly never be fully understood by outsiders. Nevertheless, this book silences those voices that still dare to deny or trivialize the Holocaust.

From Auschwitz with Love reveals the true nature of Nazi torturers: sadistic, scornful and brutal. They starved, dehumanized, humiliated and punished their victims. They lied to them, using cynical and cunning euphemisms[1] and incessantly disguised their sordid acts. They were self-satisfyingly cruel and administratively outrageous.

The Jews knew of the gas chambers, the crematorium, and the Sonderkommando; some even caught a glimpse of these crimes against humanity. Others were naive, many couldn't believe what was happening to them. Nonetheless, they continued to hope and desired so badly to live. Yet this hope could not keep everyone alive. Others who were too weak to bear such abject horror ended their lives by throwing themselves onto the electrified wires surrounding the camp.

At the end of the war, Manci and Ruthie still had to endure a Death March. It was an absurd, nonsensical march aimed at preserving the "market value" of the victims. Many died before the Swedes liberated them. With the help of an uncle and aunt, Ruthie and Manci managed to reach the United States, their haven, their paradise.

Manci and Ruthie have both rebuilt their lives, creating strong relationships and warm family ties. Their determination, their joie de vivre, and their *will* helped them overcome their loss and devastation and allowed for their integration in America. Ruthie has spoken of her deportation, as has Manci (although more reluctantly). Their narrative relates significant facts, invaluable for historical accuracy.

Daniel Seymour's work is rigorous and remarkable, adding yet another genuinely honest and personal account to defend the truth about the Holocaust against false news and misinformation. His work is well documented, having consulted many works by a variety of researchers and historians.

Many testimonies of prisoners in Auschwitz have been written, this book enriches such accounts in its precise description of the sisters' memories. Their mutual caring and their strong family ties created a mindset that undoubtedly saved them. These eye-witnesses, victims of Nazism, have grown old and their lives grow more precious. Their combative spirit is the guarantor of the power of reason and universal values.

During those dark years in the 1940s, I was a Jewish child too, and although I lost a number of family members, I was lucky because I was hidden and because my parents survived. I am immensely grateful to Daniel Seymour, not only for his serious research and his careful gathering of documents, but for this moving and reliably true presentation of the Holocaust.

- Danielle Bailly, *Professor Emeritus Paris-Diderot,* Editor of *The Hidden Children of France, 1940-1945: Stories of Survival* (*translation: Betty Becker-Theye*)

PS. Since French is my mother tongue, I would like to thank Nancy Vermès, for her kind help with the foreword.

---

1. Cf. Victor Klemperer, *Lingua Tertii Imperii*, traduction Elizabeth Guillot, Postface Alain Brossat, Coll. Agora, Pocket, 1999 (1st edition 1947).

INTRODUCTION

This book is a love story. Manci and Ruthie Grunberger are two sisters in a family of ten who lived in Mukacevo, Czechoslovakia (later to become Munkacs, Hungary after being invaded in 1938), a small city at the base of the Carpathian Mountains of eastern Europe. In their youth, they were lucky enough to experience the natural form of affection that flows between parents and their children. Surrounded by siblings, grandparents and cousins in a secluded pre-World War II environment, this love was embedded in who they were and the persons they were to become later in life.

The entire Grunberger family — grandmother, mother and father, uncles, and eight siblings — was sent to Auschwitz during the Holocaust. Only Manci and Ruthie survived. The sisters met three other girls in Auschwitz — their cousins Edith, Magda and Kis Magda — who managed to endure camp and an ensuing Death March together, recuperated together in Sweden, and then never let go of each other through their subsequent journeys in life — another kind of love.

Upon their arrival in the US, the sisters first found protection in the safe and welcoming home of an aunt, Katie, and her husband, Harry. It was a little piece of Mukacevo that enabled them to move on with their lives. And that "moving on" came in the form of two young men who would become their husbands. Ruthie married Ernest Mermelstein and, in the same year, Manci married Kurt Beran. In both cases, the love was characterized by fierce loyalty and enduring bonds that lasted more than six decades.

There is also a higher form of love, that the Greeks referred to as *agape*, or selfless, unconditional love, involving endless compassion and infinite empathy. Total acceptance transcends individual flaws and personal shortcomings. The sisters, Manci and Ruthie, embody this type of love, not because of what they endured but because of the persons they became.

They became two remarkably successful women who chose very different pathways through life with, in some cases, competing values and dissimilar interests. And yet, because of their selfless love, their bond as sisters has only grown stronger as the years and the decades passed.

The process of putting together their story did not follow a short or straight line. It has been 40 years in the making. I was first introduced to Manci Beran when my girlfriend, Rhonda, took me home to meet her parents. With Rhonda's father, Kurt, I had a lot in common. He had been in the army as a career officer, and then went back to school at the University of Oregon to get a Ph.D. He was teaching at Oregon State University when we first met.

I was following a similar path by having been an enlisted marine and then returning to college with the eventual idea of going to graduate school. I was in the same Ph.D. program at the University of Oregon as Kurt when I met Rhonda.

Manci was working at the time. As I recall, she said she was Czech but there was never much discussion of her background. She spoke with a thick accent. It wasn't until much later that Rhonda mentioned, almost casually, that Manci had been in a concentration camp during WWII. That was where the conversation was left.

When we were married in 1983, it was the first time I met Manci's sister, Ruthie, and her husband, Ernest Mermelstein, who traveled from New York to be at our wedding in San Francisco.

Over the years, Rhonda and I moved to the east coast and back to the west. I had a fairly normal relationship with the family — with Manci and Kurt, and with Rhonda's sister, Sandy, and her husband, Tracy. There were holiday, birthday and anniversary gatherings and trips to Vancouver, Canada, where Sandy and Tracy lived with their three children, Lauren, Cameron and Emma.

In the late 1990s, Ruthie sent Rhonda and me a copy of her book, *Beyond the Tracks: An Inspirational Story of Faith and Courage*. I have the signed copy on my desk today. Around that same time, Sandy sent us a video of an interview that Ruthie had done with the Shoah Foundation in her Brooklyn home a few years earlier. It was riveting to me because it made the words in the book so much more powerful. For the first time, I had a limited understanding of what Manci and Ruthie had been through as children and teenagers in war-ravaged eastern Europe. It also made Auschwitz and the Holocaust much more real to me.

My knowledge, however, was incomplete because it all came from one sister, the sister who had chosen to speak and write about her experiences. It was at that point, nearly 20 years ago, that my interest in Manci and Ruthie's story was piqued. The story that some knew in the family was important on a very personal level. Ruthie's children, David, Evy and Zvi, had a shared experience, and that experience was being passed along to their children in the stories about their dear *bubbe*.

But the question that gnawed at me was why Manci, my mother-in-law, had not shared her story even among her own daughters. Of course, it was her story to tell or not tell. No one had the right to make any sort of judgment or inference about that. And besides, who was I to attempt an incursion into such a deeply private and understandably traumatic set of events?

The issue was never really about the specifics of their experiences. I assumed that, while incredibly tragic, it wasn't necessarily different from the wave of other humans who were subjected to the horrors of the Nazis. Also, thanks to the incredible work done by researchers at Yad Vashem, the United States Holocaust Memorial Museum, the USC Shoah Foundation and the brave stories shared by Elie Wiesel, Viktor Frankl and many other survivors, that important written and visual history has been carefully documented. My interest, instead, was on how these two young girls had not only survived their ordeals but actually thrived into adulthood by creating their own personal futures while always remaining deeply connected to each other.

In 2017, Kurt Beran, Manci's husband of nearly 70 years, became ill. As Rhonda and I spent more and more time at home with Manci in San Diego, I sensed that our daily chats had turned more reflective. So, at some point, I broached the subject: "Would you be willing to talk to me about your life?" While she did not enthusiastically embrace the idea, we decided to just start and see where it went. I began by asking whether she could tell me about growing up in Czechoslovakia.

There were some fits and starts, but there came a time when the actual recording started and the questions became more explicit. It was never really easy, but — just like other aspects of her life — once she decided to talk about her experiences, she proceeded in a fully engaged way. Later, Ruthie agreed to speak with me as well, and there were times when the three of us sat at the kitchen table and just talked.

Ultimately, I would say that this story somehow emerged rather than that it was planned. The individual narratives, the connections and the divergences revealed themselves as Manci's interviews took place and the full meaning of Ruthie's written words were given context. The most powerful narrative force, of course, was when the sisters spoke to me together. The essence of selfless love was on full, beautiful display.

Each section of this book has an historical or informational overview giving context for the sisters' individual narratives. There is no attempt to provide anything close to an exhaustive accounting of events. Indeed, the effort is a mere snapshot that is intended to offer some of the basic facts so that the sisters' stories can more easily stand on their own.[1]

Manci and Ruthie's narratives are organized the same way throughout the book. Manci begins each section and then Ruthie follows, back and forth. The timelines are comparable and the events themselves are intermingled.

It is important to note that the narratives themselves are entirely the voices of the sisters, with only very minor editing and additions to help with transitions. Manci's memoir materials came from only two sources. The vast majority of Manci's stories comes from the many interviews I conducted with her individually and in combination with her sister. Ruthie's narrative comes from interviews as well and from other materials including her *Beyond the Tracks* book and her Shoah Foundation interview.

Memoir materials taken from these sources remain verbatim, although they are not cited as such, with one important exception: diaries they wrote in Sweden after they were liberated are cited in the memoirs. Within days upon being freed from their SS guards near the border with Denmark, the sisters were helped by the Red Cross to Sweden. They were emaciated. So the immediate help involved food and nutrition as well as beginning physical rehabilitation. But they were also in quarantine and the Red Cross knew the advantage of offering mental health support as the liberated groups came into the country. One tool was to encourage them to write down their experiences and feelings in a diary. Such a diary was entitled "Journal of Recollections after Liberation" or known as a *naplo* (diary) in Hungarian. Ruthie started her *naplo* by writing: "Only two days have passed since I stepped over the gate of freedom," while Manci began with: "I am starting to write this on the first day of my freedom; that is, May 1945." They both, obviously, were reflecting on their newfound freedom, and that is why diaries like these have such emotional immediacy.

Ruthie's *naplo* is almost 30 pages. Manci's is much shorter. In my interview with Manci she said, "My diary in Sweden; I stopped after five pages because I couldn't handle it. I just couldn't do it. I got that far and couldn't go on." Indeed, it is important to observe how quickly the sisters chose different coping mechanisms that allowed them to thrive in their future lives. In my first interview with both of them together, they said:

Manci: "Okay, Daniel, we can talk for a little bit about our lives. It doesn't seem like anything interesting. People went through so much worse. Ruthie, you know you should start, because you keep talking about things, so you remember them better."

Ruthie: "I wish I didn't remember."

Manci: "I know. I lived it but you live it."

I had access to a fairly unique compilation of photographs. Most Jewish families were marched out of their homes at gunpoint, clutching only a few items. As a consequence, many family pictures were lost forever. The sisters were fortunate to have had Aunt Katie.

Over the years, photographs of the Grunberger family made it out of war-torn Europe, across the Atlantic and into the safety of Katie's home in Philadelphia. Katie and Harry not only became the guardian angels of their traumatized nieces, they also became the custodians of many of the photographs.

I had a singular luxury. Manci and Ruthie were scrupulous editors of their own stories. They employed sharp pencils when reading early drafts and had, of course, final say.

It is my hope that these memoirs of Manci and Ruthie remind us of our special obligation to reflect on the causes and events surrounding the genocidal rampage of Nazi Germany. "Never again" needs to be embedded in the values of modern humankind so that we remain clear-eyed about what we are capable of at our worst.

It is also my hope that their moving stories reflect on the best of who we can be. Perhaps Viktor Frankl, a survivor of Auschwitz, too, said it best: "Everything can be taken from a man but one thing: the last of human freedoms — to choose one's attitude in any given set of circumstances, to choose one's own way." Manci and Ruthie Grunberger from Mukacevo, Czechoslovakia, survived as a single spirit and yet chose their own ways to thrive: *From Auschwitz with Love.*

- Daniel Seymour, Palm Springs, California

Family picture at Ancsi's Bar Mitzvah in 1937 — Emma Grunberger (left), Ruth (left, back), Manci (middle, back), Ansci (right, back), Esther (front, left), Baruch (front, center), Nuti (front, right), and David (father).

---

1. The reference materials for each of these sections are provided in the Sources section.

PART 1

NEVER WANTING
1925-1937

Mukacevo was a city in Czechoslovakia that served as the commercial capital of a region — Subcarpathian Rus — of eastern Europe that lies between the Carpathian Mountains in the north and the Hungarian plain. Prior to World War I, the region was part of the Austro-Hungarian Empire. Upon the collapse of the Empire, the region became part of the new Republic of Czechoslovakia. Mukacevo remained under Czech control until 1938 when, after the First Vienna Award, Hungary annexed southwest Subcarpathian Rus, including the town of Mukacevo, which became Munkacs (Hungarian).

An important characteristic of life in Subcarpathian Rus was its relative isolation from the rest of Europe and, indeed, the world. Other than lumber, the region had few natural resources, and there was limited industrial development. While the surrounding areas were largely farming and logging, the city of Mukacevo had banking, law and medical practices as well as various mercantile trades.

The region was ethnically diverse. The majority population consisted of Ruthenian (ethnic Russian or Ukranian and either Greek Catholic or Orthodox) but also Magyar (ethnic Hungarian), Slovak, Romanian, German, Czech, Polish and Roma populations. Jews were a large and growing part of Subcarpathian Rus, and Mukacevo was the most important Jewish community in the region with 40 percent of its residents being Jewish.

The Jewish community itself was quite fragmented. Most Jews adhered to a traditional religious lifestyle in contrast to Hungarian Jews, for example, who identified more as Hungarians. In addition, Munkacs was also home to a thriving Zionist youth movement. A Hebrew Gymnasium was the crown jewel of the Zionist education system. By 1938, the school had 390 male and female students.

No significant antisemitic tradition existed in Subcarpathian Rus, with relations between Jews and the diverse ethnic communities being described as "placid" prior to the Hungarian annexation in 1938 and World War II.

Strabichovo

September 25, 1925 — Manci

I was born on a farm in Strabichovo, Czechoslovakia in 1925. When she was about to give birth, my mother, Emma Berger, traveled from Mukacevo where we lived to where her parents lived in Strabichovo. A year earlier, my older brother, Anshel — we called him Ancsi — had also been born there so that my mother would have the support of her family.

The town was only 15 km southwest or about 30 minutes from Mukacevo by train. It was right next to another small town, Gorond. Going back and forth at that time wasn't any problem — there were no borders, nor guards or papers — even though it was disputed area since the end of the Austro-Hungarian Empire after WW1.

The farm in Strabichovo where I was born belonged to my maternal grandparents, Chaim Moshe and Pepe Berger. It was a large farm and they employed sharecroppers — people who worked the farm. It was the second marriage for both of them. My grandfather had three children with his previous wife and my grandmother had one, Katie, who had emigrated to the United States years before I was born. Together they had three boys and my mother, who was the youngest child of the family.

My father's name was David Grunberger. It was the second marriage for my father's parents, too. He had four brothers, all from the first marriage, and a sister who died before I was born. I never met my real grandmother, Manci, after whom I am named.

Together with two of his brothers, Mordechi and Sigmund, my father owned a wholesale grocery business in Mukacevo. Eliah, a third stepbrother, was not part of the business and lived in Ilosva, which was south of Mukacevo where he had a lumber yard. We would go there to visit him and my cousins.

I adored my uncle Shmuel. He lived in Nyiregyhaza, Hungary where he had a grocery business similar to my father's. Sometimes I went there for my vacation. Uncle Schmuel was married but didn't have any children, so maybe that was why he loved when his nieces and nephews visited. He had a terrific sense of humor; he was always laughing.

In addition to four brothers, my father had one sister named Giza. She got married and lived in Beregszasz, a place close by, to the south of our city. We would visit her, too. Aunt Giza ended up having a family of five daughters and one son.

My mother and father were married when he was 23 and she was 18. We lived in a big house on Danko Street, in the same cul-de-sac as my paternal grandfather and his wife. Although we lived in Czechoslovakia, we spoke Yiddish or Hungarian rather than Czech. Depending on the conversation or who was visiting, my parents were

Mammy and Tatty in Yiddish or the endearing form of Anya and Apa in Hungarian — Anyuka and Apuka.

I considered myself very lucky in those years with wonderful parents and a large family with grandparents, uncles and many cousins. There was hardly ever a meal with just my parents and us children; our dining table was always full with members of our large family.

Before 1938, when the Hungarians annexed our part of the country, we led a very simple, very peaceful and uneventful life. There is not much to talk about it because, looking back now, it seems like it is how children should grow up.

Mukacevo

February 27, 1928 — Ruthie

I was born in Mukacevo, Czechoslovakia, on February 27, 1928. My parents already had two children: my brother, Ancsi, who was four, and my sister, Manci, was two and a half years old.

My parents named me Regina Rella, but I never really liked Regina. By the time I was in school I was called Rella. My Jewish name was Rivka and it was difficult to pronounce, so everyone called me something different and I would start crying. Manci used to call me Ipi.

I was a very fat baby and was always sleeping. My mother used to sit and listen to me breathing to make sure I was still alive. I never cried and had to be woken up for my feedings. My face was so chubby that my eyes were squinted shut. I loved food and my parents were always trying to put me on diets as I grew older. I really envied Manci who could eat anything she wanted without getting fat. As she grew older, she was still a very skinny girl, and Mother used to feed her fattening foods and fish-liver oil, but nothing seemed to help.

Mukacevo was the largest city in the area but still small. It seemed to be evenly divided between Czech and Hungarians, and many others, too. But maybe one-third were Orthodox Jewish, and they were a very close-knit community.

Distances were such that we could walk to anything. There were two bakeries in our street. We brought our kugel and cholent to the bakery ovens on Friday and picked them up before Shabbos lunch. There was a grocery store on Yiddishe Gasse where children could buy potluck packages and inside were candy and toys. Such a treat! The fish store and *shlocht hoize*, where people brought their chickens and geese to be *shechted*, was also on Yiddishe Gasse.

Across from the fish store was the mikveh and another large building, a bathhouse we called the Spa. It was for women only and we would sometimes go on Sunday. There were a few pools, each with water of a different temperature. Afterward, you could shower, stretch out, and then they wrapped you in sheets.

The shoemaker shop and *shaitel macher* were situated on Galus Street, as well as the kindergarten we attended. My mother's cousin was the teacher. The Czech elementary school that I attended was located on Zrinyi Street. All the teachers were nice to the Jewish students.

There were no Bais Yaakov or Orthodox elementary and secondary schools for girls in Mukacevo. We had a tutor who taught us the Hebrew alphabet, *aleph beis*, and how to *daven* or pray. On Sundays there was a Bais Yaakov group, which consisted of maybe 20 girls around a long table, and our teacher, Rivka Nanie, taught us Jewish history, reading and *davening*.

I had a lovely childhood. I cannot remember ever wanting anything that I didn't have.

David Grunberger, the Grocer

1929 — Manci

I was around four years old when I remember going to my father's work. *David Grunberger, Spezerei und Colonialwaren Grosshandlung* imported tea, rice, almond, coffee, and pepper. My father, Mordechi and Sigmund distributed their goods throughout the whole area. They had three stores, but the main one was on Masaryk Street with apartments above the store. Mordechi lived there with his wife, Basche, and they did not have any children, so I stayed there every now and then. He was a gentleman, very soft spoken. During Yom Kippur I was staying with Uncle Mordechai, and I had scarlet fever. One is supposed to fast, of course, but the doctor said I had to take the medicine. After father and uncle had gone to the rabbi to get his permission, my aunt and uncle really spoiled me rotten the whole time I was sick.

Each of the three partners performed a different role in the business. Father was the boss and took care of bookkeeping while Mordechi did the crating and helped others with delivering. Uncle Sigmund (we called him Uncle Shia) must have been in charge of sales because he was always traveling.

Their store on Masaryk Street was almost like a tunnel. It was so big and seemed to go on and on when I was a little girl. The business didn't cater to the public, so it was just rooms with barrels. In the back were offices where my father and a helper did the bookkeeping. Usually there were people who helped with sorting and driving. Then there was a large yard outside that was two blocks long. It even had a garden that Aunt Basche planted.

The only time we could go to father's store was Friday. The other days were too busy getting orders out, and the men would be busy loading. We would go to the back and fill our pockets with peanuts and chocolates and raisins. It was such a treat.

The store was always closed from two to four o'clock. Sometimes father would stay at work and we would bring him food in a thermos, consisting of three containers stacked on top of each other. My little sister, Ipi, and I loved to take him food at the store because we would go for a walk with Father after the meal.

We even had a truck, but I never sat in it. It was strictly for business because the distance was so far to the little towns. My father delivered groceries all the way to the Polish border. It wasn't just a business for Jews — they sold to everyone in the area. Even though it was wholesale, sometimes the priests would shop at our store and we were very friendly with them. At other times we visited their place across the river Latorica. While father spoke to the priests, we used to eat grapes from their garden.

Everyone liked my father; he was so kind to everyone and always listened to his customers' problems and needs.

Our maternal grandparents, Chaim Moshe and Pepe Berger at their farm in Strabichovo when Aunt Katie (back row, center) visited from America (1937).

David Grunberger and Emma Berger's engagement photographs (1920).

Mother with baby Esther, Nuti (front), Ruth (left) and Manci (1930).

Our paternal grandfather, Chaim Shlomo (center) with brother Eliahu and Shmuel, in Mukacevo (circa 1935).

Manci in her Royal Hungarian Business Academy uniform (1944).

The Most Beautiful Girl in Mukacevo

1932 — Ruthie

I very well remember when my mother gave birth to another girl, Esther, in May 1932. She was a beautiful baby, and had blonde hair and big blue eyes. Everyone always said that she would grow up to be the most beautiful girl in Mukacevo.

Nuti, my baby brother, had been born two years earlier, in June 1930. He was a very good baby and would never cry. In April 1934, we had another baby, Baruch. He had dark eyes and beautiful curly blond hair. When he was a toddler, he loved to roll a hoop down the sidewalk. He would forget about time playing his little games with friends and would often get scolded for being late to dinner.

There was always excitement in the house when Mother had a new baby. When I was old enough, I would help her dress, bathe and feed the little ones. One of my greatest treats was taking the baby outside for a walk in the family pram. It had been passed down from one baby to the next. I would greet the neighbors with pride and joy.

I also looked forward to helping Mother prepare for Shabbos by kneading the dough for challah. I felt such happiness as we all sat around the dining room table listening as Father would recite the *Kiddush*. We sang *zemiros* and talked. I was just so happy being there as a family.

I can still see the reflection of the 18 flickering candles burning brightly from my mother's shining silver candelabra, creating intricate patterns on the walls.

We always had guests. There was a large yeshiva school in our city and some of the smaller communities in the area would send their boys to it. These yeshiva boys had places to stay, but families in

Mukacevo would feed them in their homes. Each family would have a day, so, once a week we would have them around the table, too.

Stores were closed in Mukacevo for Shabbos, and people strolled in the main street wearing their Shabbos finery. My friends and I would get together on Shabbos afternoon at each other's homes, playing different games — even-odds with walnuts or seeds, a bowling game or playing with dolls. I often took my younger siblings — Esther, Nuti and Baruch — along so our parents could rest. Before we went to sleep on Friday, Manci and I would lay out the boys' Shabbos clothes because they would go to shul very early the next morning.

We had such respect for our parents. When Mother and Father would take a nap on Shabbos afternoon, we would all walk around on tiptoes and whisper to each other to not wake them. If we played outside in the yard during the summer when the windows were open, we would speak very quietly in order to not disturb them. I was just so fortunate to grow up in a very happy family.

Polgari

1935 — Manci

I had gone to a regular elementary school for four years and then to middle school for another five. I couldn't wait to go to middle school, or *Polgari* as we called it. It was mandatory to attend public school for nine years. After that it was up to you to study further, but girls didn't usually go on. There were Czech, Hungarians and Jewish students at our Czech school.

The city of Mukacevo was famous for its schools. Little villages around it sent students to the schools in our city. Mukacevo even had an excellent Hebrew Gymnasium that was known throughout the region.

My cousin from Strabichovo, Hendu, was five years older and she had gone to *Polgari* in Mukacevo. I was just starting school there when she was graduating. She was so smart and clever and I just wanted to stay in school and be like her.

My best friend, Frici, was eight months older than I was. Her family was not well-to-do, and her parents were much older. Her two older brothers were her protectors and they loved their little sister. Although she lived quite far away from me, Frici came for dinner at our house a lot. It was almost as if my parents adopted her. She would always come for Saturday night supper, then we would walk to her home and talk. If we got to her house and we weren't finished talking, we would turn around and walk back, until our story was finished.

We were in school together all the way from kindergarten to grammar school to middle school, and then we even went to business academy together and graduated at the same time years later. Frici and I were always the top students. Either she was number one and I was number two, or I was number one and she was number two. She was just as crazy about school as I was. Maybe that is why we were best friends all those years.

I loved school. I loved everything about it. The grammar school had been just a block away from our house. The *Polgari* was a bit further, but still within walking distance.

The middle school was very structured and difficult, with a lot of studying and homework. I don't think I ever came home without my notebook containing homework for school the next day.

We were taught in Czech, but when we were at home we spoke Hungarian and Yiddish. My parents were born before 1918 when the area was still part of Hungary. All of the older people spoke Hungarian and there were many Magyars — ethnic Hungarians — in our area. Then there were the people outside of Mukacevo. These Ruthenians spoke something else and were, I think, Greek Orthodox with Russian or Ukrainian backgrounds. They were very rough, almost backward, who mostly lived to the north in small, scattered farms that extended to the Polish border. They would come to town to sell food and buy from the shops. The Ruthenians were different, but it didn't matter because the people lived well with each other.

Zrinyi Street

1936 — Ruthie

I was very excited when we moved into our new house. When I was little, we lived in a house on a cul-de-sac where my grandparents lived with us. When the family grew, we moved to our own home, a big house with eight rooms, with the main entrance on Zrinyi Street.

Our L-shaped-house was surrounded by a wooden gate. There was a large courtyard with a narrow garden on either side where Mother grew many beautiful flowers. She loved flowers. Another part of the building was rented to two businesses — a grocer and a tailor.

You entered our house into a vestibule. To the right was a kitchen with a sink and indoor water supply. The kitchen table was very special, converting into a bed for the maid. In the hall was an ice box and then a separate cold-storage room. One thing we didn't have was a bathroom. Instead, we had an outhouse in the back. There was a woodshed and a vegetable garden in our yard with a chicken coop. On the left was a large dining room with tables and chairs, a couch and a bed. There was a closet, too, and a tile stove. A beautiful feature of the house was a gray marble *netilas yadayim* area where we could wash our hands according to religious rituals. Down one side of the dining room were bedrooms and the master bedroom at the end with a crib set up there.

For a while we had tenants, one of whom drove a taxi which he could park in a covered area attached to the house. As the family continued to grow, the house became very crowded with the four of us sleeping in the dining room. Finally, Father asked the tenants to leave because we needed the space.

We always had a maid, who was my mother's helper. None of us were spoiled, although the maid would braid our hair and polish our shoes. The maid would help Mother in the kitchen and make the fire in the morning. We weren't allowed to ask them to do anything for us.

I remember one, Bella, who was with us for a long time and used to sing us lullabies. She stayed with us for five years after which she left to live with her sister in Belgium. Another one was Sarah, who was with us for four years until she got married. Afterwards she would often visit us, taking along her own children.

We also had a Christian girl named Piroska. I liked the way she combed my hair in the morning before school. Everybody's shoes were polished and lined up. She also made a fire in the morning. Later, in 1943 or so, we sent her away because Father was afraid for her safety; he thought having a Christian girl as a maid would be a real problem.

Three times a week — Monday, Wednesday and Friday — was *marktug,* or market day, when farmers came to Mukacevo from neighboring villages. When they passed by our house we would buy fruits, vegetables, and eggs from them.

Many of the Jews were shopkeepers — textiles, furniture, and dry goods. Some were tailors and bakers. The farmers bought goods from them and then went to their homes to tend their farms.

Everyone in Mukacevo lived well together when I was younger.

PART 2

GROWING STORM
1938-1944

In September 1938, following the Munich Conference and its subsequent agreements, the Sudetenland of western Czechoslovakia was given to Germany. Several months later, Hungary annexed Mukacevo and surrounding area in the southwest Subcarpathian Rus. The Hungarian army entered Mukacevo on November 10, 1938.

Many Jews, especially the older generation, responded favorably to the restoration of Hungarian rule based upon memories of the Austro-Hungarian regime prior to the end of World War I. However, the new Hungarian authorities began to subject Jews to discrimination and persecution almost from the very beginning.

A Hungarian gendarmerie force was permanently assigned to Mukacevo which was then called Munkacs, and Hungarian authorities began imposing various laws such as limiting the number of Jewish students in schools and confiscating businesses that were owned by Jews and non-Hungarians. Harassment and persecution of Jews — especially bearded men — became common in the streets of

Munkacs. Beatings and robberies were regularly condoned. Arrests for minor infractions and grueling interrogations spread quickly.

The idea of a "Greater Hungary" — the return of territory lost after WWI and a drive to eliminate minority populations — reached a frenzy when Hungary formally aligned itself with Nazi Germany as part of the Axis Powers — Germany, Italy, and Japan — in 1940. It participated with Germany in the invasion of Yugoslavia and the Soviet Union the next year.

Many young Jews were conscripted to forced labor within the ranks of the Hungarian army. In addition, the Hungarian authorities used the war efforts as an opportunity to implement large-scale deportations of refugees and Jews who lacked Hungarian citizenship through Subcarpathian Rus.

Following the stalled war effort against the Soviet Union, Hungary attempted to forge a separate armistice with the Allies. In response, German forces entered Hungary — its erstwhile ally — on March 19, 1944. Within weeks, the Jews of Munkacs and surrounding areas were forced into two brick factories that served as ghettos. The Nazi's Final Solution program — the extermination of European Jews — was about to begin.

The Parade

November 1938 — Manci

I was 13 when the Hungarians came. While the rest of the world seemed focused on Germany's demand for more territory, Hungary pushed into southern and eastern Czechoslovakia, including Mukacevo. There was a parade, and some people — mostly older — brought out old flags and waved them as the Hungarians marched into the city. I guess they must have recalled something good about being under Hungarian rule.

At first, my mother was excited because her best friend from the time she was growing up — Maria — returned and they were reunited. Mother used to talk about "Marika" all the time. They had gone to school together in Strabichovo, but Marika had left years earlier. She was now married to a Hungarian gendarme with two children. He was even in the parade — at the front as a flagbearer!

There wasn't much change, initially. I was finishing my third year in *Polgari*. I wanted to stay in Czech school with my friends and teachers, but that wasn't possible when every school was shut down. My father said that I either went to the Hungarian school or nothing because there were no other options. So I went, and it was very tough. I had to unlearn my grammar and everything. But by the end of the year, I was the number one student.

About the same time, my cousin Hendu came to live with us. She lived in Strabichovo which was now occupied by Ukranians. We used to go back and forth all the time to see my grandparents and uncle and cousins. Since the border was now closed, we were required to obtain passports in order to visit them. Hendu was going to school and she couldn't travel all the time from Strabichovo, so she moved in with us.

I wanted to continue school after finishing the mandatory public school. My father encouraged me. He had always been more open to things, perhaps because he traveled. The rest of my family wasn't as open. My older brother, Ancsi, stopped after the mandatory years and then went to yeshiva. He loved studying the Hebrew ancient books, the Torah. My sister, Ipi, didn't really have a chance to continue once the Hungarians took control.

My cousin Edith's father, a rather traditional man, was really against me continuing my education; he thought I should get married and have children. But my father stuck up for me and said, "If she wants to go to school, then she can."

I had to take an entrance exam, and the next year I started at the Royal Hungarian Business Academy, the same school Hendu attended. One of the first changes was that only six percent of students could be Jews. It was Frici and me and a few more Jewish girls. Initially, I made some new friends as families were coming back from Hungary — then, of course, to the city being called Munkacs.

Changes were happening around us. At first, these changes came gradually and I was probably less aware of what was taking place — like the rest of the world — because I had my school. I always had school.

Szalona on My Lips

1939 — Ruthie

I was ten years old when I first experienced antisemitism. I had gone to Czech school for four and a half years before I switched to a Hungarian school for the final half year. The Czech school had only been a block away. The new school was across the street but farther away. While there were new students, many of my classmates I had known for years were there, too.

One day at lunch, three girls held me down and rubbed ham — *szalona* — on my lips. They laughed when they did it. I was shocked and scared. One girl of the girls, Metzger Emma, I knew well. In fact, I had known all of them — we had been friends.

In a relatively short period of time, the Jewish community became the target of abuse. It started as just harassment such as pulling men's beards and hitting them. Even though the Hungarians had taken control of Munkacs, there was gunfire and bombing nearby. The Czechs were fighting the Hungarians on the Orosvegi Bridge, three blocks from our house on Zrinyi Street. Refugees were pouring into Munkacs, with many from Poland after the Nazis had invaded their country. And there was more intimidation, too. The Hungarians began confiscating things by setting new rules all the time. Of course, the religious Jews would continue to go to synagogue but when they came out, the soldiers would follow them, spit on them and beat them. They found any excuse to bully them and steal their personal belongings.

Mother was very brave. When they were harassing Father one day, Mother came out and told to them, "You must be tired. You've been out all night." She then gave them some whiskey, distracting them from what they were doing. They forgot about Father. Then they began taking and closing Jewish businesses. Despite everything, our parents tried to be hopeful. They were always focused on keeping us together and trying to be normal. We were told that things were bad, but they would get better, although it seemed our suffering and of those around us increased every day. We prayed, tried to find peace and calm, supporting each other and our shul.

On September 27, 1939, my mother gave birth to a baby girl, Tobe Tobcsu Rose, who we called Rozsa in Hungarian. She was a very big baby; the doctor weighed her at 12 pounds. Her birth was especially joyous, since the year before my paternal grandfather had died and Mother had had a stillborn child.

I was so happy to have a new baby in the family, yet at the same time we were afraid of what the next day would bring. We had each other, but it was becoming so uncertain, so difficult to be hopeful.

The Lady of Mandalay

1940 — Manci

I had seen the book, *Gone with the Wind*, being advertised at the library. It had been translated into Hungarian and was called *The Wind blew it away*. I took it home and was immediately taken by it. I could not put it down because it was full of American history. It was so fascinating to someone like me and what was going on at the time. My mother used to come and check on us, but I had a flashlight under the covers, and read it all straight in 36 hours.

Between my new school and access to books and movies, I was very interested in the larger world beyond Munkacs. Frici and I were renegades. We wanted to see the movie, *Rebecca, The Lady of Mandalay,* in Hungarian, the book of which we had both read. One needed permission from school and your parents to go the movies. And even then, you were only allowed to go maybe once a month. The school was very strict and didn't allow any distractions from the lessons.

We had one movie theater where they showed American movies, some Hungarian movies and German movies. They had translations, subtitled in Hungarian. We saw all the Paula Negri movies who was Polish and my favorite actress.

So, we snuck into the theater to see *Rebecca*. There was a separate entrance to the balcony and we hid there. It was a matinee and there weren't a lot of people. I cried my heart out watching the movie. When I came home and my mother asked what was wrong, I had to lie to tell her why I was crying. I could not do that. Going to the movies without permission was a big sin. Understandably, they were very angry with me. My parents were strict and during that time and in my family, you did what you were told to do.

Frici's parents weren't as strict. They were older, and she was really brought up by her brothers who were good to her. As I have said, my father was nice to her, too, and treated her just like she was one of our family.

Ipi was finished with school by then. She was much more interested in what our mother was doing. She liked to cook and to help mother by babysitting the little ones. And she had so many friends; everybody loved her. Every holiday — Rosh Hashanah, Yom Kippur

— she would be doing chores for my mother. Her favorite holiday was Passover. She even helped with cleaning during holidays.

Our grandparents lived only a few blocks away. After my grandfather died in 1938, Ipi would always stop by, on her own, to visit my grandmother. She was sick and alone. So, Ipi would sometimes sleep at her house to keep her company.

That same year, my mother had a stillborn child. Everyone was heartbroken, but none as much as my sister who loved children so much. When the baby was lost, it really bothered her a lot.

There were so many horrible things going on that good things — like a book or movie — made it seem okay. We had such a nice life. I didn't want to think things could get worse and so I naively thought they would get better.

Nobody Believed Her

1942 — Ruthie

I hated the way the gendarmes bossed people around. They pulled Jews' beards and pushed them down. They had these hats with big feathers that made them feel bigger and tougher.

One day, they came to Father's store, confiscated his merchandise and put a Christian person in charge of it. Suddenly, Father and his brothers no longer had a business to go to. He became very depressed. Despite everything, Father occupied himself with learning, davening and helping others in any way possible. Mother tried to offer him hope and encouragement, saying it would get better. Thinking back, I don't think she truly believed her own words.

We weren't permitted to have radios, but my uncle had one hidden away. Sometimes the men would go and listen to it. But again, we were just hoping it would get better, hoping that someone would rescue us or that things would change back to how they were.

Then more refugees came, people came from Poland, and they were telling stories of what was happening there. There was one woman that I kept thinking *What a poor woman!* Something had to be wrong with her since she was telling stories about Jews being killed. I felt sorry for her. It was going in one ear and out the other for me and others, too.

My uncle even had a maid. She had gone back to Poland years before, but she came back after the Germans invaded. She told us that the Germans were killing the Jews. But, again, nobody believed her because that simply wasn't possible. I don't know what happened to her. I guess she stayed in Munkacs and was taken with the rest.

One of the things that the gendarmes had taken was black pepper from Father's grocery business. It was a very popular wholesale item because it was used in many favorite dishes. For some reason we could not know at the time, a year or more later, the black pepper was returned to him. Father saw the black pepper as a gift from heaven and sold it within the community and to Christians as well. This brought relief in the form of unexpected income for our family, because we'd had to live on family savings after the business had been seized.

But the relief was temporary. We soon found out that Father's name had been placed on the Hungarians' Black List. He was faced with trumped-up charges of hoarding black pepper. It seemed that the pepper was returned to him so they would have a reason to arrest him later.

Mother's family had the farm in Strabichovo, so it was legal for us to have sacks full of flour that came from there even though it was rationed. So thankfully, we never ran short on bread.

To the Border

1942 — Manci

I hated those people who were suddenly the new bosses. It was the lower class. They didn't have any power before, and then suddenly they were in charge. They would beat Jews and others for no reason, just because they could. And they made new rules all the time about who could go where and what you could do. We were a well-known family, accepted in the community. We had good relations with everyone, and then suddenly we were just trash.

Hendu had come to live with us. They were sweeping up Jews and others who weren't deemed Hungarian. By this time there were refugees streaming into Munkacs from everywhere. They were trying to escape the Nazis and the war all around us.

One day, Hendu got arrested. We didn't know what to do. My mother went to her friend Marika, whose husband was in the gendarmes. There was also the principal of the school who really liked Hendu. She was such an excellent student. The three of them — mother, Marika's husband, and the school principal — got a car, and together they followed the transport that was probably going to a labor camp. They finally caught up with the train at the Polish border. Somehow, Hendu spotted my mother from inside the boxcar and yelled out to her. Marika's husband helped my mother free her and bring her back. It was a miracle.

That was around the first time the Brownshirts came for Father and took him to a work camp. They always found a rule that was being broken or a new law that was being disobeyed and harassed the elite first and well-known people. They took the doctors, the businesspeople. They always came with false pretenses so they could have something on you and then confiscate stuff. There was continuous harassment.

They were the big shots now, always demanding things. We started to stay home more and tried to avoid them, but it didn't matter. They had power and they just didn't stop. They never stopped.

When a little girl was born it was customary that she got her ears pierced. My grandparents gave me my first earrings when I was a little baby. They were rubies with little diamonds that screwed on and locked. I was so proud of them. The gendarmes came to the house one day and just ripped them out of my ears and left me bleeding. They were the boss. They did anything they wanted to us. It didn't matter what you said or how you acted. They said what they wanted and took what they wanted. They were, to me, the scum of the earth.

Kohner Castle

1943 — Ruthie

I had to watch as they dragged Father away again. He had been put on a list because of trumped-up charges about confiscated black pepper from his business. They took him to Kohner Castle, which was not too far from our house and had been turned into a prison. They beat him up and after two weeks they let him come home. His ulcers were bad. On Yom Kippur, the most holy day, Father had to stay in bed because he had to sip water. He liked to listen to me pray, so he asked me to do that. He would show me where to start. I will never forget the way he listened.

Then he was taken away again. They always had false pretenses, some excuse to harass you or take you away. This time they took him to a mill called Monopol. I knew where it was. So, one day I said I was going to go watch outside of Monopol and that maybe I could see him. After a while, I did; he was taking heavy sacks of something from one place to another. He had a small beard, but they shaved him anyway. I cried hysterically because I thought that was the worst thing they could have done to him. They beat him up. The Hungarians — the gendarmes — were just brutal. They were disgusting to all the Jews.

We remained home with Mother, constantly worried over his well-being. I hardly recognized him when he finally returned. He was battered, broken, and his soiled clothing hung loosely on his skeletal frame. We still had access to food, so Mother tried to fix his favorite meals but he had trouble consuming food. His ulcer was worse, too. She tried to cheer him up, but he was too depressed and didn't talk a lot.

The hardship for everyone had grown. Often our doorbell would ring, and destitute people would ask for money or food or milk for their babies. Some would ask for clothing. We were still moderately independent because of Father's savings, so Mother would hand out some coins. Sometimes she would go through our drawers and decide that we no longer needed some things, bundle them together and give them away.

There were soup kitchens that Mother sometimes used to cook at together with other women. The tables would be set nicely so they wouldn't feel like it was charity. People felt humiliated having to go there, but there were many refugees and many businesses were shut. There were no jobs, so there was no money to buy food. People were literally starving.

Dash to Budapest

March 19, 1944 — Manci

I had been to Budapest several times. Often when my father went on a business trip, he would take one of the older children with him. Both Nuti and Ipi had been there. He enjoyed taking us by train and see the towns along the way. We would stay in a hotel, and I knew all his business partners. Some had kids my age, so it was fun.

By this time things were getting worse every day. More and more people were coming into the ghetto from outlying areas. Our house was full of relatives and friends. Soup kitchens were set up, and my parents would go and help there, too.

One day, my father came to me. He was so serious. He could not leave the ghetto, but he said he had documents for a friend in Budapest. They were in a sealed envelope and he asked if I would go with Hendu to deliver them. I think the man may have been a lawyer. He wasn't Jewish, but I know that I had met him before.

Hendu and I went. The date was March 19.

I was still in school, so I wore my academy uniform and a hat showing the holy crown of Hungary. Hendu had already graduated, but she wore her hat, too. No one would have known we were Jewish by looking at us. We didn't have any papers, but no one questioned us. We had school IDs and the train tickets. That was all.

We met him in the lobby of a hotel. He read the papers and just said something like, "It doesn't make any difference." There wasn't really much discussion. He seemed to just dismiss whatever was in the documents and sort of shrugged as if he didn't have any ability to do anything. He was very concerned about us, though. He said we needed to go home right away. There would be another train that day, the last train, and he insisted that we should be on it. In fact, he took us straight to the train station. And he was right.

We got on the train and left to return to Munkacs. We did not know until a few days later that the Germans had invaded Hungary the next day. We would never have made it back. We would have been checked on the train. Two Jewish girls, without any papers; we would have been arrested and taken away. Who knows what would have happened to us?

At the time it didn't seem like everything was getting worse, but nevertheless everything was getting worse.

Little Peska

1944 — Ruthie

I was so afraid. We could be taken away at any moment, yet at the same time we thought the war could end because of what we heard about the Allied forces. We prayed, but we did not know our fate.

On January 20, Ancsi's 20th birthday, Mother gave birth to her eighth child, a little girl, Pesel. We called her Peska. It was late at night and Father was away, so Manci took Mother to the hospital. I am not sure where he was. Maybe Father was at a work camp or trying to help other family members or friends.

She was a beautiful child. I helped Mother take care of her. She was like a living doll to me, and she brought some semblance of happiness into our otherwise tense household. One day, Father wanted to give me something for helping with the baby. Although Jewish stores were almost all closed, there was a black market. Father got a beautiful material with butterflies — *lepke* — on it. He was going to take it to a seamstress to make a dress. Unfortunately, that never happened.

We prepared for Pesach that year in our usual manner and enjoyed two Seder meals, which were led by Father. We were thankful to be together; we had our family and were still hopeful that somehow it would all be over soon so that we could resume our lives.

A few months earlier, my brother Nuti had had a problem with his foot. A bone was growing and coming through the skin. He was in the hospital in Beregszasz which had a good doctor. He was getting better, but had to stay in bed. The doctor said that he could stay with him, at his house. He probably knew more than we did and was trying to protect him. However, Mother declined the offer. "Wherever I go, my children go with me."

One day, we came home and both my parents were inside the floor-to-ceiling furnace. They had crawled in and were trying to hide jewelry and gold coins. Mother was determined that the gendarmes wouldn't get her wedding band and engagement ring. She knew that one of these times they would find them, so she carefully buried them in the garden next to the home.

The Germans arrived in our town a few months later. There was no wild rampage — just the pounding noise of their boots as they marched down the main street. Behind the soldiers, heavy tanks followed. We quickly learned that the Jews were to be banished to ghettos, and the SS began rounding up Jews from surrounding villages and towns and forcing them to Munkacs. Soon there were so many people arriving with their horses and carts piled high with their belongings.

At first, we were relieved that our home fell within the ghetto walls. A cousin and others moved in with us. It was terribly crowded, but we were terrified to leave the house.

Then we were ordered to wear a yellow star on our clothes.

Frici's Blue Dress

April 1944 — Manci

I was still in school and my schedule hadn't really changed. Frici and I had taken our final exams but not our orals. We were the top two in the class, and my father was so proud of both of us. I was even dreaming of continuing my education. The closest university was in Ungvar, which was several hours away but had also been annexed by

Hungary along with Munkacs. I wanted to study Economics. But everything around me had changed.

The Christian students, even those who had been friends — some of which I had tutored — distanced themselves from us. I had one school friend whose mother had a delicious *Konditorei* — an elegant pastry shop. I would eat at her house sometimes, not meals but cakes and stuff. I never told my mother, of course. Then that stopped. We were still in school together, but there was no outside contact anymore.

I had another friend, who I was tutoring her on the side, too. I really liked Kristofori. We went to school together in the academy from the first day, and it was almost graduation now. So, for four years, we were together. Her family had a business — something like plumbing, because they installed the indoor water in houses. Kristofori's mother was antisemitic. She said to me one day that she would be willing to save things for us, that she would keep any valuables safe. I knew she just wanted my new coat for her daughter. My father had coats made for Hendu and me. They were brand new, with Persian fur collars. They were so beautiful.

Everybody was trying to gain and try to get ahead at the expense of others. It was horrible when it happened among friends that you had known so long.

Graduation from my school — the Royal Hungarian Business Academy — was a big deal. There was a main thoroughfare in our town called "The Korzo." It was the promenade, where people would go in the evening. Every store would have a picture of the graduating class on display in their front window. They would keep the pictures up until graduation.

We had to have a navy-blue dress for the graduation picture. Frici's family wasn't well off and couldn't afford it. My father went and got the material for both of us on the black market. He then went to the seamstress and had the dresses made.

Frici was so excited and we were included in the graduation class picture. We sat together in the second row with four other Jewish girls. But I still hadn't really finished and had to take my orals that were scheduled for April 28.

The Brick Factory Kalush Telep

April 28, 1944 — Ruthie

I knew that every day the news and events were worse and worse. Robberies, killings, the Jewish shops being sealed — and we were forced to wear yellow stars. Jews were only allowed on the streets until 6 p.m. Really awful things were happening to girls, so Manci and I and the other girls did not go outside. We were trapped inside our home.

I had never seen a German SS soldier before they came to our door. They knocked but quickly kicked it in. They were looking for Father and my brother, Anchi. They said if they didn't show up in a few minutes they were taking us.

They didn't wait very long, though, and we were told we had to go immediately. Mother reached for a package on the table and a soldier with a bayonet slapped her in the face. We managed to grab some things, a few blankets and a valise of things for the baby. We were led out at gunpoint. There were horses and wagons outside homes along our street. The luggage was put in a wagon with the small children, and we were told to start walking. It looked like a funeral procession to me. I have shivers even now if I think of that.

People lined the streets to watch the spectacle. Some spit at us. Others threw rocks and yelled obscenities. We had never hurt these people! All the time we had been their neighbors, and yet they were so mean to us.

There were two brick factories in Munkacs. We were taken to Kalush Telep. They put us in a cold cellar with cement floors. We were there overnight. The next day they told Mother and Manci and me to come to the office where they interrogated the three of us. Then they sent us away, keeping Mother by herself. An hour or so later she came out and was all beaten up. Her face was swollen and she looked so terrible. Manci saturated a rag with water from a tap and washed the dried blood from her face.

After a few more days in the cellar, they said we could find a place with the others. We found a little corner; the space was tiny but wasn't as cold. The air, while stale, was better than the musty air in the cellar.

Of course, our main concern was for Father because we didn't even know if he was alive. But then a man from shul said he had seen Father in Kalush Telep, and also our uncle and our brother. When they brought him from interrogation, we could see he had been badly beaten. He stumbled and his face was bloodied. My mother tried to clean him. It broke our hearts to see him this way, but we thanked G-d he was alive.

Life in ghetto confinement was difficult and humiliating. There was no privacy because thousands were interned with us in Kalush Telep. Father and my brother would go and find food and bring it back to us. There were only a few toilets in the ghetto. You stood in line for hours, waiting your turn.

PART 3

DESCENT INTO DARKNESS
1944

On May 11, 1944, the first deportations from Munkacs to Auschwitz began, and on May 23 the last deportation train left.

The Auschwitz concentration camp complex was the largest of its kind developed by the Nazi regime. There were three camps. Auschwitz I, the main camp, was used for forced labor and targeted killings. Auschwitz III, or Auschwitz-Monowitz, was also forced labor for the manufacture of synthetic rubber and fuels. Auschwitz-Birkenau (Auschwitz II) had the largest prisoner population — divided into ten sections separated by electrified fences — and also contained the facilities for a killing center. Four large crematorium buildings were constructed, which used Zyklon B in their gas chambers. They housed eight gas chambers and 46 ovens capable of disposing of 4,400 corpses a day.

It is estimated that at least 1.3 million people were deported to the Auschwitz complex between 1940 and 1945. Of these, 1.1 million were murdered. The vast majority of these people were Jews (1,095,000 deported and 960,000 killed). Other victims were Poles, Roma and Soviet prisoners of war, as well as other nationalities.

With the deportations from Hungary between late April and early July 1944, German plans to murder the Jews of Europe achieved its highest efficiency. Approximately 426,000 Hungarian Jews were sent to Auschwitz, with 320,000 of them sent directly to the gas chambers at Auschwitz-Birkenau. Gassing operations continued until November 1944. Soviet forces reached the Auschwitz camp complex in mid-January 1945.

Yad Vashem's central database of Shoah victims' names includes the following for the family of David and Emma Grunberger of Munkacs, Hungary:

First Name	Last Name	Birth	Residence	Fate	Place of Death
David	Grunberger	1897	Munkacs	Murdered	Auschwitz, Camp, Poland
Emma Teme	Grunberger	1902	Munkacs	Murdered	Auschwitz, Camp, Poland
Asher Anshel Ancsi	Grunberger	1924	Munkacs	Murdered	Auschwitz, Camp, Poland
Nute Leib Nuti	Grunberger	1930	Munkacs	Murdered	Auschwitz, Camp, Poland
Esther Etyu	Grunberger	1932	Munkacs	Murdered	Auschwitz, Camp, Poland
Baruch Buji	Grunberger	1934	Munkacs	Murdered	Auschwitz, Camp, Poland
Tobe Tobcsu Rose	Grunberger	1939	Munkacs	Murdered	Auschwitz, Camp, Poland
Pesel Pepe	Grunberger	1944	Munkacs	Murdered	Auschwitz, Camp, Poland

The Unknown

May 18, 1944 — Manci

I departed into the unknown with the rest of my family on May 18. A year later when we were recovering in Sweden, the Red Cross asked us to write our thoughts in a diary. I wrote about this day: "My life's black day."

We had been at the brick factory, Kalush Telep, for three weeks. We were completely sealed off by barbed wire fence. Behind the fence stood the brown-shirted Hungarians and SS soldiers with their guns. We could get food and water, but that was all.

It didn't take long before the factory had been filled and whereas there were thousands of us, they continued bringing people in. The public toilet required long waiting, with the smell being horrible from body odor and excrement and vomit. There was no privacy in the situation. It was so demeaning and degrading. I kept thinking: I am a student with my oral exams that should have taken place on April 28. This couldn't be happening.

Father was broken and bloodied. I couldn't even see his eyes because they were so swollen. He was trying to be calm and telling us that we were together and to not worry. It would be alright, he kept saying.

We were told that the SS would be emptying the whole ghetto and that we would be sent to a "resettlement camp." They said that families would remain together and that conditions would be better there. Of course, we wanted to believe. It was too difficult to imagine the worst; we needed a reason to hope.

Mother tried to pack our few possessions along with as much food and water as possible. Everyone tried to help. Ipi was very good with the baby. We had our clothing and some bedding and rucksacks. And then we waited and waited for whatever was to come.

There were several transports. At the designated time we were marched out of the brick factory and into the street. Just like weeks before, there were townspeople — our neighbors — lining the street to watch us pass by on the way to the train station. Some laughed, others yelled and cursed, and some spit and threw stuff at us. The soldiers pressed us forward. They would slap people and hit them with the butts of their rifles. Babies were screaming and children were crying. Although parents tried to keep their children quiet, it didn't seem to matter. We were fortunate because our sweet little Peska was so good and quiet.

We were still together, all of us. But at some point, they started separating out the sick and elderly. My younger brother, Nuti, had not recovered from his foot injury. Also, my Uncle Mordechai was very weak. We were told that they would be more comfortable in a Red Cross car. I know it was difficult for my parents to let them go, but they hoped it would be better for them.

After they were gone, our family group consisted of mother, father, my paternal step-grandmother, Tova, my older brother, Ancsi, who was 20 years old, and Ipi who had just turned 16. And then there were Esther who was 12, Baruch who was ten and Tovah was five. The baby was just four months old.

Again, we were told that we were going to a resettlement camp where we would all be together. They said it was a better place, a place for children to play, and young people were going to work. A year later I wrote in my diary: "How could we have been so naive?"

It was all a lie. It was so horrible and unbelievable, but it was all happening. The transports began to move.

Peska Meets Hendu

May 18, 1944 — Ruthie

I saw a long line of cattle cars as far as the eye could see. Shabby wooden ramps were set up to walk up into them and the SS immediately began loading us.

The cattle cars were small, with between 85 and 90 people squeezed into each one. We were able to find a corner, though we were surrounded by sweating bodies and swinging limbs. Father was praying. The smaller children wrapped their arms around Mother's waist. She tried her best to comfort them and to reassure them.

Even though it was daytime, it was dark inside the car. The only light came from the openings between boards that were covered with barbed wire. Nazi soldiers lined the ramp surrounding the train. I was close enough to a crack to be able to look outside. Some of the soldiers saw me looking through the crack and laughed. Then there was a loud thump, and I realized we had been locked inside. Some people gasped, some cried, and others remained silent. Next, the train jerked forward, stopped and then started again slowly. Fortunately, the baby remained asleep on my shoulder, even though I must have jumped from the sudden noise. We were underway.

Once the train would be moving, I thought that at least the air would circulate, but the movement didn't seem to help much. The air remained stagnant and there was nothing we could do. A few minutes later, though, the train came to a sudden halt. Someone standing by one of the cracks looked out and read the sign: Shajovitch Telep. We had reached the other brick factory in Munkacs, and we wondered why the SS had decided to stop here.

Like my sister, Manci, I wrote in my Red Cross diary a year later and explained that: "All the Jews from the surrounding villages were brought to Shajovitch and Kallus in Mukachevo. They collected the mothers, children and parents and transported them with wagons to those awful places. All my relatives from Strabichovo and Iloshva were there."

I was close enough to be able to see outside, and after a moment or two I saw, Hendu. She was in a huge crowd of people surrounded by soldiers. I called out to her and she turned her head in my direction. Looking over her shoulder to make sure she was not being watched by the SS, she ran over to our boxcar and looked in.

I was so happy to see her. My cousin Hendu hadn't been living with us for a while, so she hadn't even seen little Peska. I was holding her at the time. I tried to turn my shoulder and show her the baby's angel face. Her reaction wasn't what I expected; she seemed so sad. Instead of smiling or wishing *mazel tov*, her face became sullen while her dark brown eyes filled with tears. She turned and walked away. I asked Manci, "Why doesn't she make a fuss over the baby?" I think she knew that to live under these conditions was so horrible. I guess she knew what was coming and couldn't be happy.

Again, the train pulled out and I tried to get one more glance of my cousin as we left. But it was too late; she was already lost in the crowd.

Soon we rode past the brick factory, then out of Munkacs as the train picked up speed. Before long we were in the countryside where there were trees and wildflowers. I saw farmhouses and cattle roaming the fields, and little children running and playing in tall grass. For them, it was a day no different from any other.

I looked at my own little brothers and sisters and saw the anguish on their distressed faces as they stood in the wretched boxcar. They hovered in fear next to my parents, who really could not offer them much comfort. They looked so pale, so terrified. I thought of little Peska who remained asleep, and wondered what kind of a life she would have.

Zombies

May 18-21, 1944 — Manci

I don't remember much. We were like zombies. It was impossible to comprehend what was happening at the time. It wasn't that long ago we were in our home with family. Things had gotten bad, but we had still been able to get food and our father still had had money for things. We had been able to move around, too. Now we were packed into cattle cars with no air, and we had to urinate in the corner. The stench was horrible.

We had taken some food along, but water ran out quickly, and there wasn't any inside. We were all thirsty. The lack of water was especially difficult for mothers and their babies. The mothers were having trouble producing milk and the babies were crying. Once one or two started, it seemed that they all began crying. It produced a sound that was heartbreaking.

On the second or third day, the train stopped and the SS ordered us out. It was a lovely landscape; the trees were in bloom, the sky was blue, and the birds were chirping. There was even a spring breeze. It didn't seem real; it was more like a painting we had stepped into.

We had a few moments to relieve ourselves but there was no privacy. We squatted by the side of the tracks. We briefly saw Nuti and our Uncle Mordechai. Even though my mother had nourished Nuti to help the healing of his foot, it never completely got better. He continued to walk with a limp, and felt pain after being upright for any length of time. They both looked pale and bathed in sweat.

It was only for a moment it seemed and then they ordered us back on the train. We were pushed and shoved. The soldiers shouted and cursed at us for no reason. They beat those who did not comply quickly enough.

And then we were back, mostly standing because there wasn't really any place to sit. It was so exhausting and numbing. Again, I was in a daze. Everyone was, from the heat and the lack of air and the swaying of the train from side to side.

Ipi was very good with the baby. She would sing a lullaby to her and try to rock her to sleep. My father would pray softly while my younger siblings would cling to mother.

I do not know when my grandmother died. Tova was old and frail. Maybe it was on the first day or maybe it was a day later. A lot of people died on the train. Tova's husband, my mother's father, had died four or five years earlier. He owned a saloon and one day some Hungarian soldiers had come in and beaten him. A few weeks later he was hospitalized in nearby Beregszasz, but he never recovered. He always had this dream to die there where his parents and siblings were. And so, his wish had come true.

Maybe it was better that way. He didn't have to see what was to come, what was to happen to his family — to his wife and children and grandchildren. Everything was taken away. There was nothing left of the life they had built when Mukacevo was a quiet city in Czechoslovakia. After it had become Munkacs when the Brownshirts poured in and then the Nazis, it would never be the same.

In the corner of the boxcar was everything we had. Our family was there with some food, some clothing and bedding in several rucksacks. Mother had some sugar water for the baby. No one else — our friends or cousins — were on our transport. Hendu and Frici were taken later. We did now know that we were earliest because of Father. They first put the people on transport they knew had respect or influence, and could quickly confiscate their property.

The train moved on.

Later in Sweden, I wrote in my little diary: "A three-day tortuous train trip. Ninety people in one boxcar. The children are weak, everyone is fainting with thirst. My mother is terribly upset. Little Peska is sick."

Auschwitz Station

May 21, 1944 — Ruthie

I was holding the baby when the train stopped. It was dark and quiet when we arrived at our destination in Poland: Auschwitz Station. This was supposed to be the resettlement camp. There was activity, lots of activity. We could hear it. And through the slates of the boxcar we could see fire in the distance — flames coming out of huge chimneys. What could it be? Factories? Perhaps iron works or coal refineries?

We waited. There were so many cars and so many people. Suddenly the sliding doors to the cars were thrust open and hordes of Nazi soldiers surrounded by skinny men dressed in striped uniforms screamed at us to get out, quickly. What we saw is something we will never forget. I later wrote: "They let us out of the wagon at ten o'clock in the evening. There is a wire fence all around and it is lit well like some big city. German officers are standing everywhere."

They shouted over and over, *"Raus! Raus! Schnell! Schnell! Los! Los!"* They used clubs and whips. There were screams and blood as people tried to shield themselves from the brutal blows. There were dogs, too, vicious-looking and tearing at our clothes and flesh.

Behind us, the kapos — the veteran prisoners in striped uniforms chosen by the Nazis to keep their fellow prisoners in line — were busy emptying the train of bodies. Many elderly people and children were among the dead. Some little infants were still wrapped in blankets. My grandmother was among the dead.

Cries of the *Shema,* the Jewish plea to G-d for His help, rang through the air, piercing the dark night. This was followed by more blows from the soldiers and the kapos, punishing us for saying prayers.

Immediately, men and women were separated. There was no time for farewells; besides, I thought that we would all be together at some later point. We were ordered to stand in line five abreast and march along a hard dirt path. I continually blinked from the intense light coming from the large floodlights. They produced an eerie sound — one could almost feel the electric current. There were elevated guard towers and high electric fences with ominous warning signs: "Beware! High Voltage!"

Waves of fear, then panic, overcame us as we continued to march along. My sister Manci tried to comfort us. It was difficult to see beyond the fences. There was darkness on both sides. Finally, we saw a long building silhouetted against a fiery red sky. We followed the path to the building and remained in line, with women on one side and men on the other — again, five in a row.

I scanned the men's line trying to locate Father and my brothers, but to no avail. There were thousands of men and many SS soldiers and kapos surrounding them. I later wrote: "My little brother Nuti has come in with the hospital train along with my uncle. The hospital train was not sorted. It was sent directly to the other side. As long as I live and I see a car with a red cross, Auschwitz will come into my mind."

As we stood there, I couldn't take my eyes off the red bursts of flame spewing from a brick chimney. What could they be burning at this time of night? There was a foul odor in the air and heavy dust particles drifted in the night breeze. I was puzzled over the white haze that surrounded us. We walked on a hard dirt path which was filled with small patches of overgrown grass and wild weeds. There were waves of fear, then panic, that overcame us all as we continued marching at a pace set by the SS.

The Selection

May 21, 1944 — Manci

I wrote my first impression of Auschwitz later: "We arrived Saturday night at the Auschwitz Station, but we waited for 24 hours until our turn came to detrain. For this was Auschwitz's busiest season. They came by the thousands, no, the tens of thousands."

I just wanted to breathe. My initial reaction was just to be reprieved from the hot and cramped cars that we had endured for three days. What it meant to experience the suffocation, the horrible heat in the cramped boxcars, one cannot express in words.

We said goodbye to Father because we saw and knew right away that the men were separated from the women. We were being pushed toward a group of SS soldiers.

I know how young he looked, the SS officer who was standing at the front of the line facing us, women. He was handsome and was dressed immaculately, including white gloves. He was making a motion with his gloved thumb: You go left. You go left. You go right. You go right. Just like that. Most of the women and children were selected to go to the left, only a handful of them to the right. Many families were being separated and they were screaming and crying while soldiers pushed them hard and yelled loudly.

All of a sudden, Uncle Shie's daughter Edith appeared near us. Our cousin was 15 years old. Ipi was holding the baby, and one of the striped uniforms said, "Every mother holds her own baby." Reluctantly, Ipi gave Peska to Mother. When our turn came, my mother, the baby and the other children were sent left while Ipi, Edith, and I were given the signal to go right. We didn't know what it meant. What did left mean? What did right mean? We were so frightened at the thought of being separated because we had been huddled together trying to be strong and not to think of the worst.

When Ipi realized that she had the small suitcase that had some items for little Peska, she ran over to mother to give her the bag.

The SS officer grabbed Ipi first and then looked at my mother. I'll never forget what he said to her. "You are so young. Why don't you give the baby to someone else and go over here with them?", referring to Ipi and myself. He wanted mother to go with us for some reason. She was beautiful, had perfect features, and was only 42 years old, blue-eyed and blonde, and she looked innocent with pure skin.

He was calm and mild-mannered. But mother would not let go of her baby or leave the small children. It was just like with my father and brothers, we thought we would be reunited. We thought that eventually we would be allowed back together. Again, we had no way of knowing what the different lines meant — left versus right. What could it mean?

As my mother moved away, we began to march along while glancing over our shoulders and back to the right. We quickly lost sight of her and the younger children.

I had seen the Red Cross cars earlier. We assumed that Nuti and Uncle Mordechai were here, too, even though we hadn't seen them. We had lost sight of Father and Ancsi when the men were separated from us. Now mother, the beautiful Esther, Baruch and little five-year-old Rosza were gone. And, of course, Peska was taken away, too.

There were only three of us left together: Ipi, cousin Edith, and me.

During the following days it were the other inmates who almost matter-of-factly began to tell us what was really happening. It was just hard to imagine they were telling us the truth. It was simply too horrible. And it wasn't until even later that we were made aware of the name of the young elegant SS officer who had done the selection that sent my mother and our little sisters and brothers to their deaths: Dr. Josef Mengele.

Gone Forever

May 21, 1944 — Ruthie

I had forgotten about the suitcase for the baby and ran back across to Mother. I was grabbed by the SS officer. I stood there as he spoke to Mother, telling her in a regretful tone that if she had not been carrying a baby, he would have selected her to go with the women on the right. "Dort werde ich noch einmahl sortieren," he told her: "There I will select again." But she wouldn't leave her baby.

It was a moment of agony that I wrote in my diary, "I realized that I was holding Peska's suitcase with all her things. I went fast to give back the suitcase to mommy but the officer didn't let me. I begged him. The baby looked back with her big blue innocent eyes, and it was goodbye forever."

I crouched close to Manci and Edith and looked around to see who else was on the line with us. Somewhere behind me, I spotted a girl from our hometown, Ingber Libu, and tried to get her attention by waving. She had gone to school with Manci and graduated a year ahead of her. Fortunately, she saw us and ran over. Manci grabbed her hand, and it was a comfort to have such a close friend by our side.

We were pressed to start marching forward for perhaps half an hour while I kept looking back to look for my darling Mother and our sweet, innocent siblings as they had disappeared into the dark.

We didn't know it at the time, but they were about to enter the steel doors of the gas chambers, and within minutes, they would be murdered — asphyxiated by poisonous gas. From there, inmates of the Sonderkommando would remove their bodies and drag them to another room in which gold teeth would be extracted and hair would be cut off. Even in death, the bodies were not treated with dignity and were tossed like raw meat into metal carts.

We found out that, when filled, the carts were placed on a huge elevator which went up a floor to the crematoria. The Sonderkommandos would then shove the bodies into the ovens, and their ashes would rise along with the flames — the flames that we had seen upon arrival at Auschwitz.

Nuti and Uncle Mordechai had probably suffered the same fate. The Red Cross cars were just used so that the feeble and elderly would enter them quietly. Once at Auschwitz, they were some of the very first to be murdered. The SS had deceived them into thinking that they were being taken care of and would be safe.

We were pushed forward again, being marched to a building in the distance. Dozens of soldiers were on top of us, pushing and beating us. Their yelling rang in my ears: *"Mach los! Schnell, du Schwein! Los! Los!"* A Slovak girl, one of the kapos, told us that we were going to the showers, the sauna. We would be cleaned and then given clothes. We shouldn't be afraid, she said, and we would have our hair cut, be taken to barracks, and then be assigned work. It was an effort to calm us down, to make sure that things didn't get out of control. By then, it probably must have been around midnight.

We didn't know where we were going or what lay in store for us. We were marched to a building known at the camp as the sauna for bathing and delousing. We saw dark silhouettes of two men working alongside a fire. They would bend down together and pick up something and throw it into the fire. I heard somebody behind me say that they were burning bodies. It was a ghoulish spectacle and set a wave of fear among the girls. Others cried out, and that was all it took to set off an outburst of screaming as we reached the building.

Many refused to go forward, even with the dogs lunging and the guards pushing. Why the guards didn't shoot us right there and then, I will never know.

The Sauna

May 21, 1944 — Manci

I know that we kept looking back. We wanted to see our mother and the children, even for another glimpse, but the SS pushed us forward into the dark. They screamed, pushed, and used their rifles to beat us again and again as we stumbled forward.

I remember this day, this event, so vividly and I later wrote in Sweden, "We, in the front, were struck dumb with fear, but the 'marchers' in the back had broken out into screaming and crying, and to the surprise of the SS, no one wanted to go into the sauna. I didn't see anything, but the girls in the back alleged that they saw bodies being thrown (alive or dead?) into the fire. I was only frightened by the fiery red night sky."

By the time we had reached the building, there was an outburst. Even though we were being pushed forward to go into it, there was so much hysteria. We had, by then, believed that they were going to kill us, to set us on fire.

The SS realized that something was wrong and had to bring in extra guards. Eventually, they started using female kapos who spoke Hungarian to reassure us, and we moved to the entrance. They told us not to be afraid and explained that we would have our hair cut, go to showers, then be issued new clothes and be assigned to work. It was just to calm us down and get control over were several hundreds of hysterical girls and women. The SS were afraid of panic and rebellion.

In my diary I wrote: "Our refusal was out of the ordinary and unusual; because of this, for months people in the camp spoke about our transport. Weeks later, when we were already in Birkenau and working near the sauna, a man told me something when he learned that I was from Munkacs. He said we were the only ones who had opposed the SS." I don't think they ever brought another transport in at night after that. They would only bring them in during the day so the fires didn't create silhouettes in the darkness.

We eventually filed into the building. With men SS and women kapos present, we had to take off all of our clothes and throw them onto a pile. We were totally humiliated. Next, we were ordered to sit down, naked, on long benches. Each of us was then dragged to where the "barbers" were lined up. Our hair was cut to the roots using scissors and razors, a painful process.

Ipi had two long, thick braids at the time. It was a shock to see her with nothing but short stubble in place of her beautiful braids.

Then we went into the showers. We tried to hold hands — Ipi, Edith and Libu — when we were herded into a huge tiled room with rows of spigots attached to the ceiling. The water came out with a hard force and freezing cold. It knocked some girls off their feet. The blood from the brutal cutting of our hair swirled around with the water.

After we had taken this shower, the kapos entered and pushed us out of the shower room while the German soldiers stood there watching everything, leering and laughing.

We received rough gray dresses that looked like potato sacks. Each of the dresses had a large "X" that was painted on the back in what I remember being a green, fluorescent color. It was obvious that it was intended you could be seen in the dark. We weren't given anything else. No undergarments or stockings. We only kept our shoes from our original clothing. Then they pushed us out into a dressing room.

Usually after women were dressed, they would use a rear exit to go into the camp when the men would come into the shower. Since we had unboarded the train at almost midnight, our group stayed in the sauna until dawn.

I was very tired and stretched out on the cement floor to sleep.

David Grunberger, the Locksmith

May 22, 1944 — Ruthie

I was lucky to find Father in the crowds although I could barely recognize him. All the men who had come in on the same transport as us, and who had survived a *Selektion*, had collected on the other side of the sauna. Father was among them.

The men, too, had been stripped of their own clothes and had been put into prison suits, which looked like ill-fitting pajamas. Their heads had also been forcibly shorn, and those who had been bearded had their faces shaved as well.

My Father was very upset when he saw us. He could not get over what the guards had done to Manci, my cousin and me. He kept being so bothered about our being bald, but Manci said that it didn't matter. She was trying to keep us calm by saying, "The hair will grow back."

While Uncle Shie was with Father, I noticed that Nuti was not by his side, nor was Uncle Mordechai. They had been transported to Auschwitz in a Red Cross car, whereas Father believed they had been sent to a hospital where they were taken care of until they were well enough to work. It had been a relief to Father that Nuti didn't have to walk the mile to Birkenau. Of course, he thought he would see Nuti later but we discovered that there was no hospital. They had gone directly to their death.

Father realized that we didn't have much time together. So, he said to us, "No matter what happens, I want you to remember three things."

"First," he said. "if anyone asks whether you have a trade, say yes, and they will put you to work. If you don't have a trade here and you don't know how to work, they have no use for you and they will probably shoot you. I was a wholesale grocer. That's not considered a trade here." He knew a little something about being a locksmith, so if anybody asked him, he would tell them he was an expert locksmith. "If you should see Mama, tell her that if she is somehow able to look for me, she should look for David Grunberger, the locksmith, not David Grunberger, the grocer."

Manci and I then reminded him that we didn't have trades. He replied that Mother had taught us how to sew and cook. "If they need somebody to sew something, you know how to sew. If they are looking for a cook, you're a cook. Whatever they're looking for, that's what you are."

The second thing he told us was to eat whatever they would give us to eat. Our family had always kept strictly kosher, but we understood that he was talking about our survival.

"Finally," he said, "I want you to make sure that you are mindful of the company you keep." I now realize that he was warning us, because you would be shot for the slightest infraction. So if we were going to stay out of trouble, we would have to be extremely careful of what we said and to whom we said it.

There were many things I wished we could have said to each other, but the soldiers returned and ordered us away from the fence.

My sister and I did not know then that we would never see Father again.

"A" Lager, Block 26

May 1944 — Manci

I remember the barracks were barren. It was just to house as many as possible and looked like a long horse stable. The "stables" were jammed together, too, and all being watched by SS guards in overhead towers.

I have such vivid memories of this perhaps because I wrote about the barracks in Sweden after we survived Auschwitz: "We arrived in the "A" Lager, Block 26. One cannot imagine what these wooden barracks looked like in which 1,500 to 2,000 people lived, or rather suffered. The bunks were stacked one on top of the other. A bunk was just a little bit wider than a regular bed, in which 12 to 14 people were jammed. To stretch out, or even sit, was out of the question."

The walls had no windows, but there were small skylights in the high ceiling. On either end of the building was a door, a small entrance. The barracks didn't have a bathroom and, instead, there was a barrel outside. It was in the open so anyone could watch. With so many girls using it, the barrel had to be emptied often. There was also no tissue or toilet paper, nor a sink nearby to wash our hands.

I was very aware from the beginning about the regimen, the system. They had rules for everything but never explained anything. Things would just happen when we were in Auschwitz. For example, the kapos tattooed us within just a few days but there was no warning. It was clear what mattered to the Germans: It was the meticulous way they went about their work and there was even a roster for the tattooing. Next to the number they had jammed into your arm with ink there was a line and you had to sign your name. The SS were interested in having the records.

We got up at 4:00 in the morning and stood in the dark for several hours before we were counted. *Zeilappell!* Always counting. At night it was the same routine, maybe even longer. The SS would continually check, check, and recheck. Bad weather didn't make any difference. Even during heavy rainstorms and fierce winds, we stood outside lined up in straight rows of five and anyone standing out of place was beaten. Always head counts. *Zeilappell*.

We had tea to drink — green leaves, and usually with worms that you needed to pick out. A brick of bread divided in four was often the day's meal. Sometimes there was soup with beets and potatoes. Rotten potatoes. There was a bitter taste. It was called "brom", a drug that made us drowsy. If you were calm, you were also more submissive. We stopped having our menstrual cycles during this time, too. Something in the "brom" had that effect. But we never forgot our father's words: "Eat whatever they give you to eat."

It did not take long until you learned to accept things. You didn't worry about it. It was just a matter of getting by — day by day. Maybe the only thing you couldn't get used to was the cruelty of the kapos. You couldn't be sick. If you were at *Zeilappell* and you fainted, someone had to pull you up. Otherwise, that was it. If you were sick and couldn't work, they had no use for you.

From the beginning, you either gave in (and then you had no hope) or you decided they were not going to win. But still you never thought you would get out. We were prepared to be worked to death. And that was it because I don't think anyone ever thought they would survive.

You weren't ever going to be free, but you still wanted, deep down, to somehow live.

Kanada

May 1944 — Ruthie

I think it was only a few days after our arrival — we were standing at *Zeilappell* — when a Nazi officer came and selected several hundreds of what must have been "healthy looking" girls. We were among the ones selected. We were taken to the bathhouse again, were disinfected, and were then pushed into a line outside. When I reached the front of the line, I gasped in horror. We were about to receive tattoos on our arms. My turn came and I grimaced in pain when the kapo burned the numbers into my arm — A-5878. Manci was before me in line and was A-5877. Edith was A-5879.

My arm throbbed from the pain of the needle. But the immediate pain was replaced over time by a sick feeling of what was happening to us — we had just become numbers. During one night I tried to rub the numbers off my arm just in case we were somehow able to escape, as if only the numbers on my arm stood in the way.

We were assigned to work in a large warehouse called "Kanada" (named that, we later found out, because Canada was considered a place of abundance). Kanada was situated in the village Brezezinka, which was part of the vast sprawl of Auschwitz-Birkenau. In the warehouse clothing, baggage and other personal items that were taken from the people brought on the transports was stored. We sorted people's belongings into piles.

When I first stepped into Kanada, I was amazed at what I saw: mountains of jewelry, clothing, shoes, cosmetics, food — everything! There it all was and it became clear to me what was happening. They were stealing our possessions — cherished items and valuables to their owners — and sending them off to Germany. What had become of all these people whose possessions we were sorting?

On the other hand, I realized that we were lucky for now. Others had been assigned to hard slave labor outdoors and were exposed to the harsh elements. Working at Kanada, we had fringe benefits. The man in charge was Mr. Wertheimer who treated us reasonably well. Usually, he left us alone and did not subject us to the beatings we received from the other kapos and the SS. Because Mr. Wertheimer would "look the other way", we were able to take some clothes for ourselves — undergarments, stockings and shoes.

We sometimes made strange discoveries as we sorted the items. One day, Manci saw another inmate wearing green and white silk pajamas. She said that Mother had packed them the day we were driven out of our home. "Are you sure they're yours?" I asked her. "Yes," Manci answered. "I can even tell you where the belt is: in the pocket." And there the belt was. The girl let Manci have them.

Most importantly, we had access to food. We found assortments of canned goods, candies and dried fruits. When the SS wasn't looking, we would eat as much as we could. There were no regrets. We were following Father's advice to survive. When we ate the food — when it was available — we became stronger physically and mentally without us having to rely on food in the barracks only. Our minds were keener, too, because we weren't eating as much of the "brom."

Once the word got out to the SS that our group of girls was not eating from the camp, the soldiers marched us into our barracks and watched us eat all the soup. Soon we started feeling doped up again whenever they forced us to eat the food.

When we began our work in Kanada we had to march from Lager A to the warehouse. It was quite a walk — maybe half an hour each way. That march would have happened after our two hours of *Zeilappell* at dawn each morning. Weeks later, we were assigned to barracks right next to the warehouses. That spared us a long walk to and from work, but we were now right by the SS, so they forced us to shower every day in cold water to disinfect. Other prisoners in the camp suffered from body and head lice which spread easily, and the SS were meticulous about not wanting us to infect them.

Magda and Kis Magda

June 1944 — Manci

I met Magda early on at Auschwitz. She was a little older and educated. I was a naive thing, and she seemed very worldly and impressed me. At first, she tried to rule over me and couldn't, so after that we got along.

She was Yugoslavian and Jewish. Her last name was Friederich, but she had gotten married before she came to camp, and her maiden name was Rausnitz. The reason she was arrested was because she had been working for the Resistance when she was caught.

Magda was tough. She had been at Birkenau for a while — maybe a year — before we met and had recovered from typhus. She knew the ropes. When we first met, she was alone but a little later she met a girl from Budapest, Hungary, whose name was also Magda. She was younger, maybe about Ipi's age. So, we called her Little Magda or Kis

Magda. She turned out to be Magda's cousin, though their families were not close.

There was another girl who knew Kis Magda who tried to be a part of our little group, too. She looked like the Hungarian singer and actress Katalin Karady who was very popular at the time. But we didn't really click with her.

Our cousin Edith's family and ours weren't that close in Munkacs — in fact, I cannot ever recollect being in her house. Ipi was much closer to her because they were about the same age and they had been pretty close friends.

I know Edith was in the same transport as us but in a different cattle car. It was right around when Mengele was doing his selection that Ipi saw her — so we were selected together. She had been all alone but, after that, everyone thought we were sisters.

So, there were five of us for much of the time we were there.

For some reason, Magda had picked me out of a bunch of girls to be her friend. She was older, maybe 22, and worldlier than any of us but she became my partner. I was 18 and we were both very protective of the other three.

Ipi and Kis Magda were 16 and Edith was just 15. They didn't fight us, but Edith was always more defiant and maybe a bit more fragile. Ipi treated me as if I were her mother by then; she and Edith depended on me. So, if I managed to get a little extra bread, I would make sure they got it first.

This was our little band: two older ones and three younger ones. We stuck together.

I guess this is just how we decided to survive. We tried to stay away from others like Father said, and be careful who we associated with as far as the other prisoners were concerned. But the more difficult problem then — and still a horrible memory — was our interactions with the transports.

Both Ipi and I had the same problem and reaction. When others on transports would ask us, "Will we see our children or our daddy again?" we would answer "yes" with a heavy heart. To this day, we both feel remorse because we knew where they — and most of their family members — were going. But we believed that it was easier to go to death unknowingly than to be fearful and trembling in advance.

I would have been guilty if I had not led the girls with Magda. And I didn't have a choice because Magda was my partner. For some reason, she had decided to be my friend even though she had had such a colorful life, and I was so much less experienced. Being a small band looking out for each other had a lot to do with our keeping some hope. But every day we kept seeing the hopelessness around us because we really didn't have any real reason to believe we would survive: Everyone around us was dying.

I Know Everything

June 1944 — Ruthie

I fell into a dull routine of *Zeilappell* and work. When we first arrived, we were at "A" Lager and we had to march to the warehouses. It was quite a long walk — approximately half an hour each way. Later we were assigned barracks next to the warehouses, and to other buildings.

I know when I found out for certain. We hadn't been at Auschwitz too long. I needed to go relieve myself one day, and this meant leaving the barracks. The barrel was set up next to the building. On my way I met a woman who was from Munkacs that I had seen while we were at the brick factory. "Do you see that pile of ashes?" she asked me. "That's where your parents, sisters and brothers are." I stared at her because she couldn't have known. We had been told by others that the flames coming out of the chimneys were from burning bodies, but that could not be.

Not long after, I found out the truth.

There was a brick building close to the warehouses. It had little windows sealed with bars and flaps. One was partly open, but I couldn't see in. Soon there was frantic commotion. I could hear screaming and pounding on the walls. The voices grew loud and then I heard a mother call out, *Shema Israel*. A little child was holding the rails and crying. A moment later an SS officer hurriedly went to the window and shut the flaps from the outside. Then the sounds faded.

It was true; indeed, the woman from Munkacs was right. I wrote later, "They couldn't burn only in the crematoria. They couldn't cope with so many, so there were two open fires. From here no one ever went on to work and that is why there were three selections per day."

All the horrors that had been told were true. These innocent people, just off the trains, were being gassed to death and their lifeless bodies taken to the ovens and burned — the flames, the thick smoke, the heavy dust particles and the putrid odors were from bodies. Somehow, I managed to get back to the barracks. I was in shock and was screaming, "I know! I know everything!"

Manci raced to my side and slapped me over and over until I collapsed to the floor. Her blows stung but she understood the situation. My screams could easily have alerted the SS that something was wrong. They would have killed me on the spot and perhaps would have dragged the other girls out and killed them, too.

How would I be able to return to work?

Yet, we were determined to survive, so I knew I had no choice. Manci and Edith were badly shaken, too. I cannot tell you how, but we somehow were able to go back to Kanada and mechanically return to the sorting job.

We just did our work. It was something to distract us so that we would not have to think. We had a good kapo, and he was mostly nice to us. We had little capsules that you could light and burn, and so we made ourselves a small oven for cooking things. We would have someone outside and if the SS came, they would say, *"Geshen"*, our code word. Then we would hide everything.

We also tried to remember who we were and where we came from. One of the girls in our barracks managed to smuggle in a calendar, and therefore we knew the dates of the upcoming Jewish holidays. The High Holy Days had a greater significance to me than ever before. We prayed quietly from a *machzor* found among the clothes in Kanada. I pleaded with Hashem to allow me to survive, and to inscribe my name and the names of my family and friends in the Book of Life.

But the Nazis knew all of this and they would target Jewish holidays for their *Selektions* in the ghettos and the concentration camps. Many new transports from all over Europe arrived on Yom Kippur. And we would be outside for *Zeilappell* on those days in the morning and evening breathing our nostrils full of ash.

Shame on You

July-November 1944 — Manci

I was aware that the transports kept coming. Throughout the summer it seemed that the pace picked up. The camp was run at a fever pitch and we were even working night shifts.

There were a lot of suicides. Some of the people had been there a longer time, so maybe it was a sense of hopelessness. The transports came mostly from Hungary, Czechoslovakia and Yugoslavia. For some reason, it seemed that many of the suicides were Greek women.

We had electric fences. All you had to do was grab hold of the fence and you were dead.

The days really became a haze. *Appell.* Work. *Appell.* Work. *Appell.*

We had Slovakian women kapos. Some of them weren't too bad but a few were worse than the SS. They had to prove that they were tough because the Nazis didn't want to do the supervision. So, they were always finding times and excuses to hit you. They had a uniform and they got better food, so they closely watched what we were doing just to survive. They were always trying to impress the guards to show that they could maintain control.

I remember one called Yoli. She didn't go out of her way to hurt someone. But there was another kapo, Manci, my own name, who was from Slovakia. She was big and tall and mean. We had our numbers sewn on all our clothes. But sometimes we would wear stockings or something we had found that was warmer. One day she caught Ipi without it on a sweater that we found while sorting clothes. She slapped her really hard and knocked her to the floor and kept hitting her. She was also Jewish — most of them were — and it just seemed so awful to do. Horrible. I yelled, "Shame on you!" and she finally stopped.

The other girls would have supported me if I had started hitting the kapo back. But we just never knew how the SS would react. Sometimes they would ignore things and couldn't be bothered, but at other times a girl would be dragged out and executed on the spot.

There were things or people, however, that lifted your spirits. For example, we used the same water pumps as men in the morning because we were adjacent to a men's camp. There was one French guy who took me under his wing. We would talk, and he would slip me bread sometimes.

There was always a way to get a little extra. You did what you had to do to stay alive.

Of course, that is not the image that the Nazis wanted to portray to the world. We had an orchestra. There was a gazebo and a stage. The SS handed out instruments to prisoners who had been talented musicians before the war. The Red Cross would come in and then a "concert" would be aired over a radio to the outside world. The musicians didn't have a choice to play along because they were terrified for their lives. And then to make it truly gruesome, the stage was right next to a crematorium.

You wanted to live, but you lived in a haze. I don't know what kept us alive. I really don't. But I also had no choice because it was my job, my responsibility — along with Magda, my partner. It was what my parents, especially my father, would have expected of me.

In the fall, the camp started to change. We heard stories that the Germans were losing the war. The Red Army was coming from the east and pushing toward us. The frantic number of transports and selections during the summer and early fall started to slow way down. As a consequence, our work in Kanada slowed down, too. We didn't know what would happen to us. At least we didn't have to sort through the possessions of people who were going into the crematorium.

The killing was slowing down, but we thought that we would probably be next. The Nazis wouldn't allow us to survive: We had seen too much.

Sonderkommando

July–November 1944 — Ruthie

I thought it was a haunting feeling. Besides sorting clothes in the warehouse, we were assigned to enter the sauna building and remove clothing left behind by the other prisoners and victims. You were always wondering about the owners and how the SS lied and deceived them into thinking that their lives were about to get better.

One day, I saw a huge transport arriving with very old people, children, mothers and fathers. A man with torn shoes walked by and, by chance, the shoes fell off his feet. When he bent down to retrieve them, he received a blow from one of the SS soldiers who said, "Where you're going, you will get new shoes." The man saw me standing just a couple feet from the fence and asked me, "Is that true?" With tears in my eyes, I nodded and said, "Yes." What else could I tell him?

But of all of us the Sonderkommando had it the worst. These were the Auschwitz inmates who were forced to work in the gas chambers and crematoria. They had to remove the bodies from the gas chambers and then open the ventilators to air it out. A few moments later, they would put on special masks, open the doors and enter the chamber room. They had to wear heavy rubber boots as well, because they had to hose down the bodies. The bodies had to be dragged out and then sent to the crematorium for burning. They had to wash down the room — blood, vomit and feces would be on the concrete floor and tiled walls.

The SS bribed them with better living quarters, plenty of food and liquor, but it drove many of them crazy. They sometimes recognized the murdered people as family or friends from their own towns. And they knew they would never survive the camp. They had seen too much. At regular integrals — a few short months — their time was up. They would be lined up and shot in front of a firing squad and a new Sonderkommando crew would take over. Their first assignment was to place their predecessors into the ovens. When they weren't doing their work, they would just drink to soothe their nerves. Just like a doctor, though, they too were on call. When a new transport arrived, they had to be ready to do their work.

I once recognized a few men from Munkacs. One was Dr. Peter Zoltan who was a dermatologist. I cooked some barley and pushed it under the wire fence for him one time. Everyone was yelling because I had stumbled or something and had touched the wire. But it must not have been on. They said I was meant to be alive — after Mengele and then that.

Somewhere around October, there was a rumor of a Sonderkommando uprising. They knew what going to happen to them. Some women prisoners had smuggled in small portions of gun powder and the Sonderkommando planned to blow up the crematorium.

They were able to blow up one crematorium. The explosion reverberated all around the camp, and we literally felt the ground shake. I knew the exact time and later wrote in my diary, "It is a Friday. It is 11:00 a.m. Through the window of the barrack, I see a big black smoke and later fire. What a terrible and at the same time beautiful feeling it was to see and hear that our people also had courage."

Within a short time, the guards were on the scene. They were fighting the fire and searching for the perpetrators. One person, a Greek fellow, made it to our barracks and we hid him under blankets. But a kapo found him and she wanted to save her own neck so then handed him over to the Nazis. There were hundreds of prisoners that were shot after the mutiny was over. The leaders were publicly hung in the Appellplatz.

In the weeks after, the SS didn't believe that there was any reason for Sonderkommando to live. Mass executions started. Peter Zoltan was among them. We could hear the Sonderkommando men, brave men, singing *Hatikvah* on the way to their graves.

PART 4

ON THE RUN
1944-1945

In the summer of 1944, a massive Soviet Army offensive in eastern Belarus resulted in the first Nazi concentration camp, Lublin/Majdanek, being overrun. Shortly thereafter, the Nazis ordered that all other camps should begin preparations for evacuation of prisoners to the interior of Germany.

The major reasons for this action were, first, so prisoners did not fall into the hands of the Allied or Soviet forces to tell their stories. Also, the Nazi regime still needed forced labor to maintain production of armaments, if possible. And finally, some of the Nazi leaders were attempting to use concentration camp prisoners as hostages for separate peace negotiations with the Allies who were advancing rapidly from the west.

The final evacuation of Auschwitz was set in motion by an order issued on December 21, 1944. The instructions were to evacuate all POWs, forced laborers and concentration camp inmates and transfer them to locations in Germany where they could be dispersed for labor assignments.

The evacuation of Auschwitz camps began in earnest on January 18, 1945, with some 56,000 prisoners marching due west about 65 kilometers to a train station at Wodzislaw. Another large group marched for about 50 kilometers to a railway junction at Gleiwitz. They were joined along the way by prisoners from other sub camps. Many of those who were too sick and unfit to march were massacred by SS guards, who were also charged with destroying documents and eliminating evidence, including blowing up the crematoria. On January 27, 1945, the Soviet Army entered the Auschwitz camps and liberated more than 6,000 prisoners, most of whom were ill and dying.

During the death marches, the SS guards were under strict orders to kill prisoners who fell behind. Many were simply shot where they fell. In addition, the weather in eastern Europe during the winter of 1944-45 was particularly brutal. Thousands of prisoners died of starvation and exposure as they were being driven ahead of the advancing armies.

German forces surrendered in the west on May 7 and in the east on May 9. To almost the last day, German authorities continued their death marches.

The Decision

December 15, 1944 — Manci

I knew that things were changing. The number of transports had slowed down in the last few weeks and months. It was in the air. There were rumors about the war and we knew that the Russians were coming. We could hear artillery and bombs in the far distance in the east.

Early December at *Zeilappell*, the guards asked for volunteers. If they did not come forward, they were going to pick. For what? They never really told you anything — you just didn't know, from one moment to the next, what was going to happen. They called it a "private transport", and the person in charge was a civilian.

Magda and I were co-partners with both of us feeling like parents. I remember saying, "We are never going to get out of here. There is no chance if we stay. We aren't really taking a chance if we decide to go." Magda and I made the decision. We told the younger ones, and we all volunteered. We just felt sure that the SS wouldn't leave anyone at Auschwitz alive.

The problem was that Edith was sick. They didn't accept her at first, but we kept insisting that she was with us. We just kept insisting that we were all together.

Nothing happened for several weeks. Staying could mean that we would be liquidated when the Red Army arrived; leaving on a "private transport" could be another plan to kill us. At some point, it was almost that you didn't care. You just had to choose. Was it a ruse to take us out in small groups to be killed or whether we were actually going somewhere to work where it might be safer for us than Auschwitz?

The rumors continued, and the bombs seemed to get closer every few days.

On December 15, the five of us were loaded into cattle cars along with some 300 other girls. It was freezing. We were given an extra loaf of bread and margarine. We also had some extra clothing and we had put more paper in our shoes because it was so cold. We didn't know where we were going. They didn't tell us anything. They never did.

We stayed on the train for maybe ten days. Starting in Poland, we went all through Czechoslovakia into the mountains to Germany. We stopped a lot along the way and we ultimately lost track of time. Meanwhile, planes were flying overhead. Every time the bombs would come, the SS would hide, sometimes they went under the train. We didn't care because we figured out that they were aiming at the Germans, not us.

We kept together, though. They gave us some food, but we just seemed to be forever on the transport without knowing where we were going or what they would be doing with us.

Again, it was an unbearably cold winter. The train just kept moving forward as we moved first closer and then finally into Germany. In addition to the extreme cold, there were heavy snowstorms. We were always so cold.

Reichenbach

December 1944-February 1945 — Ruthie

I wasn't sure where we were going until we actually got there, a place called Reichenbach. In the dead of winter, we had traveled from Poland, through Czechoslovakia into Germany.

The Germans had a factory for making lamps and assorted aircraft parts. We stayed in a cold concrete building about four miles outside the city of Reichenbach, where the factory was located. The building was no more than an empty room with a concrete floor.

After a few days, we got some straw and thin blankets to share. Every morning we would be woken up at 4:00 for roll call. And then we would be marched to the factory. We struggled in the darkness with the icy-cold weather and deep snow drifts. I sometimes found myself waist-deep in the snow.

In our futile efforts to keep warm, we took paper from the factory and wrapped it around our hands and our frozen feet as we marched. It was never enough; we were always terribly cold.

Compared to what we had seen and experienced at Auschwitz, our outward existence at Reichenbach was almost "normal." We worked in the factory with civilians. We worked side by side with them but were kept under strict supervision and strict orders. We couldn't talk to them or mingle at all. Still, after spending eight months in Auschwitz, we were walking among people, children, and working along civilians.

We had real soup at lunchtime: thick soup. There was a bakery downstairs. When we passed by we would smell the delicious bread, such a wonderful aroma and what a change from the horrible smells at Auschwitz.

Every evening after work we had to make the same four-mile trek in the snow back to our ice-cold barracks. We would pass by civilians on the roadway. Some stared at us in amazement while others scowled in hatred, screaming obscenities and shouting that we deserved to die.

If the sun ever shone in Reichenbach, I never saw it.

We were there for maybe six weeks or two months, working every day at the factory and marching back and forth in the wind, ice and snow. Toward the end, there weren't enough materials for us to work with and so we stayed more time at the barracks.

It was a great joy when the girls came home to the Lager with the news that some factories in Reichenbach had been bombed. We kept thinking that we were just staying ahead of advancing Russian soldiers, and that perhaps they would free us. But then we were told that our group would be moving. Everyone got one kilogram of bread, a little sugar and a little piece of margarine. It was supposed to be our supply for four days.

This time there was no train, though, and so we were sent from Reichenbach on foot. But to where? We didn't know. We weren't told.

Each morning, we were ordered to march into the mountains through the snow. Some of the women just couldn't continue. They would sit down or fall, be shot and pushed off the road.

Trautenau to Hamburg

February-April 1945 — Manci

I don't know how many of us made it. I do know that they took all of us from Reichenbach. But this time there was no transport. We were forced to walk 25 to 30 kilometers a day through the mountains. They just gathered us up and started to march. I don't know if they thought they wouldn't be bombed, or maybe they didn't have any fuel. But we were on foot, closely guarded as usual.

Besides our group from Auschwitz, there were other women slave laborers, too, maybe a few hundred in all. We were in the Sudeten Mountains of southern and eastern Germany. The snow was deep and the cold would have been difficult even if we were dressed well. But we weren't.

We would stay wherever we could. One night we'd be in a barn, the next night in a church and then in a granary. It didn't matter as long as we could get a roof over our heads. In the morning we would be ordered to begin marching again.

One time we went to sleep in barracks where Russian soldiers were held as prisoners. But in general, wherever you were, you just laid down and slept. That was it because you were so tired. Some of the women would march as far as they could and then they would quit. They could go no farther. A shot would ring out and the march would continue.

On February 16, we arrived in Trautenau where we were put into open coal cars. After another ten days on the move, we arrived in the rundown Camp Porta. I think we were making radios or telephones; it was always something for the war.

Conditions at Porta were horrible. Within hours of our arrival, we were infested with lice. Manci, Edith and I would spend time picking the lice off one another, but we couldn't stop them. It seemed that every second of our day would be focused on the bites, the itchiness, and then the ultimate bleeding and infection from the sores. There was little or no food except for rotten potato peels. But there was a German guard who snuck food to me that I could share with Ipi and others. He was decent and he even gave me a little pocketknife with my name on it. I still have it today.

We left Porta after a month and traveled in closed cars to Bensdorf, and after that to a place called Ludwigslust. It seemed as though we were just steps ahead of the Red Army. At some point we were at a plane factory that appeared to be carved out of a mountain. The space was massive — it was filled with fighter jets, airplane parts, and different tools. We were led to worktables and ordered to assemble parts for different sections of the airplanes.

Then we were on the move again. This time we ended up going even farther north in Germany, to Hamburg and Altona. We were on a chain gang, digging ditches and fixing roads with shovels and wheelbarrows. That lasted for only two weeks or so. Then there was another SS-escorted transport for us. But the size of the transport was smaller by then because there were a lot fewer of us.

A Strange Silence

April 30, 1945 — Ruthie

I still had hope. You had to think you would survive. We still seemed to be just ahead of the Red Army. There was the bombing and the artillery. Each day was the same. From dawn to dusk we were on our feet marching, marching, marching. Our numbers dwindled as the deaths of women increased. I would watch them drop to the ground. Shots would be heard and the bodies would be kicked aside into the ditch.

We, too, were probably close to death. Our bodies had been reduced to skin and bones, and we were filthy and covered with lice. We had countless scars, reminders of where we had been beaten by the Nazis and the kapos. My knee hurt badly and I had an open wound on my leg. I realized I needed medical attention. We feared each day was the end. The SS troops wouldn't surrender and we knew they would kill us first.

I remember I had my birthday during this time, but it didn't matter. It continued to be raining and freezing as we were moved from one place to another. The blankets at some point had actually become molded around our bodies.

One day in late April, the train stopped after we had left from Hamburg where we had been digging ditches. It had been rolling along the tracks, and just as before we were crowded inside, standing in the dark. We expected the sliding door to open. But they didn't.

We waited. More moments passed, perhaps even an hour went by, and still nothing happened. A strange silence surrounded us all — an eerie silence which, to this day, I find difficult to describe.

One of the girls nervously peeked through the cracks in the boxcar and let out a scream: "Nobody is out there!" But we didn't know what it could possibly mean. Was it a trick? We always were thinking the SS would be waiting to finish us off. Or had the Russians finally caught us and our guards have just fled?

We weren't at a railway station. We were at or near the Danish border, but we really didn't know where. It was the middle of nowhere. More time passed as we continued to wait.

Finally, one of the girls slowly slid open the door. There were people running toward us. They weren't the SS guards and they weren't in uniforms or Russian soldiers. And then we realized who they were: Danes. It were people from a nearby town who were coming to help us. We bombarded them with endless questions: Was this really happening? Were we really liberated? We needed to be reassured again and again because it was so hard to believe.

It was over. We were free. It was April 30, 1945. Almost a year since we had arrived at Auschwitz. More than three months since we had begun our long march through the mountains from Poland, through Czechoslovakia, and into Germany. Our captors had simply vanished on the day that, we later learned, Adolf Hitler committed suicide.

We hugged and kissed, cried and screamed, sobbed tears of joy, anguish and sorrow. It was all so hard to imagine, like the first moments you awake from a nightmare, feverish and sweating and uncertain about what is happening.

The five of us had survived.

PART 5

PARADISE

1945-1946

After Germany defeated Poland in 1940, they invaded Norway and Denmark. The next year, Finland entered the war on the side of Germany and the Axis Powers in their fight against the USSR, hoping to regain territory lost earlier. Sweden was the only Scandinavian country that was able to remain neutral throughout the conflict.

Most individuals in occupied Europe did not actively collaborate in the Nazi campaign against Jews. Nor did they do much to help Jews and other victims of the genocide. Denmark was an exception. In 1943, upon learning that the Nazis were planning to deport Danish Jews, the Danes organized a nationwide effort to smuggle their Jewish population by sea to neutral Sweden. In less than a month, 7,000 Jews went into hiding and an underground effort led by Danish fishermen managed to ferry most of them into Sweden.

The invasion of Hungary by Germany in 1944 led to other significant efforts to save Jews. Raoul Wallenberg, a Swedish diplomat, was dispatched to Budapest in July of that year as a representative of the newly formed, US-led War Refugee Board. He began issuing "protective passports" to Jews while negotiating and bribing the German and Hungarian authorities. Using private funds, he rented buildings and designated them as Swedish libraries and institutes with large flags displayed. The buildings were then used to house Hungarian Jews. He is celebrated for saving tens of thousands of Jews in Nazi-occupied Hungary. Others such as Joel Brand, a leading figure in the Relief and Recovery Committee in Hungary, made various attempts to exchange trucks and other materials for Jewish prisoners.

The Swedish count and diplomat Folke Bernadotte also negotiated the release of prisoners from Nazi concentration camps during this period. As the vice president of the Swedish Red Cross, he led the "white buses" operation (buses driven into German-controlled areas) undertaken by the Swedish Red Cross and the Danish government in the spring of 1945 to rescue concentration camp inmates and refugees and transport them to Sweden. Although the operation was initially targeted at saving citizens of Scandinavian countries, it rapidly expanded to include citizens of other countries.

Oatmeal and a Prince

May 1945 — Manci

I know we must have been a sight: hundreds of girls, stubble for hair, emaciated and wearing rags by that point.

The townspeople didn't know who we were, and we didn't know where we were. They must have been living close by. The SS had just emptied the camp in Hamburg and so we were a larger group now. We didn't know what was happening. The people who came to us knew some German language and so they asked us who we were. We said, "We are prisoners from Hamburg."

The Red Cross came very quickly. We stayed on the train at first, but they brought us food. It was oatmeal, just oatmeal. Our stomachs had shrunk and it was too dangerous to eat a lot of rich food when you were malnourished. We had water and weak tea for dehydration.

Doctors examined us and saw how emaciated we had become. We had lice and they saw the scars we had from the beatings. We were wearing just rags on our skeletons by that point and yet we were fortunate because we could walk while many others were bedridden with malnourishment or with typhus. Ipi's knee was cleaned but it was by now ulcerated and needed to get more treatment.

They also brought us clothes, real clothes! We all got the same. They were brown dresses with white collars. I can still see my first "free" clothes since being taken from Munkacs a year ago. They brought us blankets, too. They were thick, warm, comfortable blankets. We even managed to sleep for a few hours, despite being so excited.

We were taken to a bathhouse the next day to be deloused and disinfected. They gave us thick soap and we were allowed to shower for as long as we wished. It was such a luxury. We soon got more new clothes and shoes that fit.

We even had a visitor. A Danish prince came to see us. He was a tall, attractive man, and offered words of hope and encouragement. He went out of his way to shake each girl's hand. We were all so impressed that someone like that would actually care about us.

I will never, ever let anyone say anything bad about Denmark or the Danish people. They were wonderful to us.

What I didn't know then, and still don't know, is why we were spared. Were we just slave labor? At the time we were told that we were part of some deal. Supposedly, Sweden had been trying to exchange Jewish refugees for steel. Or was it a rescue mission conducted by the Swedish Red Cross?

At the time we didn't know anything about our circumstances. But I remember it now in two ways. You either gave in and then you had no hope. Or you decided they were not going to win, but, to be honest, you still never thought you would get out.

Yet, we had really done it. We had somehow managed to stay alive through it all.

Quarantine

May-August 1945 — Ruthie

I certainly didn't have fond memories of trains. But there we were: 400 refugee girls and children sitting on a real train with comfortable seats looking out the windows onto a picturesque landscape. Freedom felt so wonderful.

After a short stay in Denmark, the Red Cross organized our travel to Malmø, Sweden. We had clean clothing, we were eating regular food, and we were all together: Manci, Edith, Magda, Kis Magda and me. It was hard to even think that only weeks ago we had been marching across mountains and digging ditches in the dead of winter under the constant guard of the Nazis.

It had been months before, when we were in the Sudeten Mountains, I had found a small bucket. Later we found some salt. So, I put the salt in the bucket and carried it all along with me. After we reached the top of Denmark on the Red Cross train, we were put on a ferry that crossed to Malmø, Sweden.

I was still carrying the bucket. Maybe it was because none of us could really believe that we were free. It was such a strange feeling. But at some point, I must have realized it was true. I took the bucket and the salt and threw them overboard. I didn't need them anymore because we were really free.

We were taken to a city called Helsingborg and placed in quarantine. We stayed in a theater that had been converted for our use as a dormitory. The area was fenced, and we were not allowed outside. Even though we were in quarantine, for us it was like paradise.

I had a bad infection in my leg that had bothered me for months. The doctors said I was lucky because it had not reached my bone. Edith was taken to a sanatorium. Something was wrong with her lungs and they weren't functioning right. The rest of us took the time to eat and rest — gaining our strength back. Many of our days were spent outdoors in the fresh air and sunshine.

Local townspeople would come and look at us behind the fence. Maybe we were a curiosity. Some would stare while others would gasp and shake their heads in pity. It was like being in a zoo.

But as the days passed, I noticed that there were "regulars" who would come often and talk to us. One man, Louis Lindholm, was very kind to me. He would bring his wife and daughter. One day, he brought me a present. Wrapped in a small box was a beautiful, delicate necklace. I still have it today and keep it in a special place.

We were in Helsingborg for maybe three months. It was lonely and we felt isolated, but we did not complain. We were safe for the first time since leaving our little town, Munkacs, more than a year ago.

The Red Cross distributed booklets when we were first in quarantine and encouraged us to write in them. The woman who helped me was Thea Bank Jensen from Stockholm. It was a *naplo*, a diary. I thought, good, now I can start writing. I actually wrote quite a lot. It wasn't easy for me, but still I just felt I had to do it. It begins: "Only two days have passed [May 6, 1945] since I have stepped over the gate of freedom. Now I am in Helsingborg in quarantine and because I don't have any important tasks I will try to write down the events I lived through in my young years. We were eight children at home..."

I will never forget the first telegram we received from the outside by the Red Cross. It was from a woman we knew who stayed in Munkacs with her husband and baby. They had been in hiding the entire time. They were alive and we were so happy for them.

Don't Move

May-August 1945 — Manci

I was given a booklet by the Red Cross. They called them the "Journals of Recollections." They encouraged all of us to write down what we had experienced as part of their rehabilitation efforts.

My diary consists of only four pages. It begins, "I am starting to write this on the first day of my freedom, that is May, 1945." The text begins with a date, March 19, 1944, when Hendu and I went to Budapest on behalf of my father. It says: "Perhaps this is when it starts."

It covers the time in the brick factory, the transport to Auschwitz and our first few days in Auschwitz. The last few lines of the diary read, "But in the first days we didn't need to eat, we were too tired and too disoriented to feel hunger. And then the first roll call, *Appell*, took place! Amidst bloody hitting and kicking, they pushed us out into the yard."

I stopped writing after that because I couldn't handle it mentally. I just couldn't do it.

We were released from quarantine after several months and were transferred to a small town called Bredaryd. We were supervised but otherwise free to do whatever we wanted. I worked for a photographer. My pay was taking free pictures. Edith joined us there after having received medical attention at the sanatorium.

In Sweden, all children under 18 were required to go to school. So Ipi and the younger girls were taken to a school in another town called Fjallgarden. Magda and I decided to move back to Helsingborg and got an apartment together. We worked in a warehouse packing Christmas ornaments. It was so boring, but, still, we were grateful for something to do.

At some point, the Red Cross had had us fill out forms in the hopes that we could connect with surviving family members in Europe or elsewhere. We knew that none of our immediate family had survived. They all had been murdered at Auschwitz. But we knew our mother had a sister, Katie, who had gone to America. She had come back to Munkacs in 1936 for a visit. She was much older than my mother because she was a half-sister from a first marriage. Her children were about my mother's age.

We were happy in Sweden and people had been so kind to us. We knew things would never be the same and we didn't know what would be next for us. But for now, we felt safe.

One day, a telegram arrived from America. It was from our Aunt Katie and her husband, Uncle Harry. They had found our names on the list that the Red Cross had been circulating. I will never forget the telegram they sent to us. It read: "Don't move. We will take care of everything."

I quit my job and left to be with Ipi and Edith in Fjallgarden. My dear friend Magda had met a medical student while we were in Helsingborg. His name was Arne and he was from Denmark. His family was friendly to the Nazis, so he left them to go to school in Sweden. They fell in love and she stayed behind to be with him.

It was arranged that I would live with a Swedish family in Fjallgarden. I was supposed to be a maid. But I spent all day with the girls at their school, and when I came home my bed would be made and there would be fruit on the table. They were so kind to me.

Refugee girls in quarantine with a doctor in Bredaryd, Sweden (1945). Ruth is center top row (light dress) and Manci (also light dress) is below to the right.

Ruth, Manci and Edith in Fjallgarden, Sweden.

Ruth and Manci at a lake in Fjallgarden.

Manci worked for a photographer in Bredyard after being released from quarantine.

The Five of Us. From left to right: Manci, Edith, Ruth, Magda, Kis Magda.

To the Opera

May-August 1945 — Ruthie

I studied English and Hebrew at school in Fjallgarden. Edith, Kis Magda and I also learned how to sew, knit and crochet and wore many of our own creations. We were taught how to apply makeup and how to style our newly growing hair.

I remember that months earlier we were working to make airplane parts at one of the work camps and I found these pieces of metal. We had our hair shaved off when we initially arrived in Auschwitz.

Toward the end of the marches, my hair had been growing out a bit and then, of course, when we were going through the mountains no one bothered to cut it. I guess I must have thought that maybe we would be rescued and my hair would grow back... and then I would need something to hold it in place. So, I made this little comb and carried it with me in my pocket all the way to Sweden.

Many of us had birthdays while in Sweden. One lovely Jewish family opened their hearts and homes to us by hosting each girl's birthday. They would make food and have an elegant buffet table and then bring out a birthday cake and we would all sing.

These celebrations were bittersweet because we missed our families terribly, but were happy to be alive and with each other.

I had such admiration for the Swedish people. They would put their milk cans outside and place the money on top of the can. They never locked their doors. They were such honest, friendly people and for the first time in years, we felt safe.

The man in charge of us at school was Eli Getreu, who introduced us to classical music. Every night when we went to sleep — there were eight of us to a room — he would put on music and gave us our own beautiful concert.

He wrote on the back of a picture he gave me, "For you to remember my gramophone playing." Mariana, a student with us, was so in love with him.

We also had a Hebrew teacher who happened to have come from Munkacs. She had survived with her mother and she even helped us put on several plays. There was *Snow White* and *The Seven Dwarves*, and we even had a masquerade party, too.

Later on, our Uncle Herman, Mother's brother who had come to the US before the war, sent us 100 dollars for whatever we needed. A fortune! We discussed what we should buy with the money. Clothes? Manci said that we could buy those later in America.

We had never seen Stockholm, though, and so we decided to go to the opera there. We had met a girl in Helsingborg who became a very good friend and who knew a lot more about Stockholm.

It was just the three of us. We took the train to Stockholm, stayed in a hotel and had a beautiful weekend.

Swedish opera was very famous in Europe. Of course, by then we knew much more about music because of Eli.

Frici Found

May-August 1945 — Manci

I would have stayed in Sweden if Katie and Harry hadn't found us and arranged to sponsor us in America. To me, Sweden was paradise. I know that I would not have returned to Hungary. It would not have been the same without my parents and siblings.

There was a lot of pressure to go to Israel. The man who was in charge of Ruthie and Edith at school, Eli, was trying hard to convince us to go to Israel. "Manci," he would say, "they need people like you." But it was an area in turmoil. I didn't want us to go from one area of turmoil into another.

Besides, maybe because my parents were Orthodox Jews, they were against the Zionists. One of Frici's four brothers, Meyer, was a Zionist. One day in Munkacs, they had a very famous speaker come and speak to a group and he was getting tickets. He asked me, whether I liked to come. I said I would. When the day came, I told my parents that I was going and they were so mad. I never forgot that. And I never wanted to go to Israel for that reason.

In Europe, you had to do everything to honor your parents, whether you liked it or not. I realized when I got older that I was not keen on tradition. At the time, though, I never would have showed it.

The Red Cross got information to Edith, too. Her father had somehow survived and had gone back to Munkacs. She didn't know what to do but she wanted to be with him. I remember the three of us — Ipi, Edith and me — having the conversation. I said, "You know you can always go home to Munkacs, but you cannot always go to America. So why not come with us? If you don't like it you can change your mind then."

She finally decided to come with us, and Katie and Harry sent papers for all three of us. Her father later came to America on his own.

We were in Sweden for almost a year when I had a dream come true. My dear friend Frici had been taken on a later transport from Munkacs. She was originally in Auschwitz, but had been immediately taken to another camp, and then to other camps. And she had survived!

She had been liberated and ended up in Gothenburg, Sweden. We were able to meet, but it was very brief. She was still in Sweden when we left for America. Frici soon began working for the United Nations Relief and Rehabilitation Administration (UNRRA) in Germany where she met her future husband, Steve, a Hungarian. I cannot recall his Hungarian name. I just always knew him as Steve.

From then on, we always kept in touch. She went back to our school in Munkacs and got our graduation pictures from the week we had been swept up into the brick factory and then sent to Auschwitz. I still have the picture of my graduating class on my bedroom wall. It shows 13 faculty members and 29 girls, of which Frici and I and three other students were the only Jews.

Frici's brothers must have been sponsored by an organization because they came directly to the US, to Harrisburg, Pennsylvania. Frici and Steve first moved to Canada and then later to Harrisburg to be with her brothers. We remained very, very close through our entire lives.

Drottningholm

March 1946 — Ruthie

I made so many friends in Sweden. The staff at Fjallgarden and my classmates were one big, happy family. After what we had been through, I could not have asked for more. By then, most of us knew that we had lost our families, although there were several who still waited for news as to the whereabouts of their parents. Now, all we had was each other, and the hope that relatives from America, Israel or perhaps even other parts of Europe would find us. We cried and laughed together, spent many hours comforting each other and offering each other encouragement.

The decision to leave Sweden, though, was not easy. My sister was the one who took care of me and made decisions for me. I felt like she was the mother in camp and so I still listened to her. Manci even convinced Edith to come with us.

Munkacs no longer felt like it could be home since everything dear to us had been destroyed. We knew that our possessions had been stolen by the SS and Hungarians. Father's business was gone. His ancient books and scrolls were destroyed or used as wrapping paper for knockwurst. Our home was gone, too. We were saying goodbye to everything we knew, but keeping our memories.

One of the guards on the staff at Fjallgarden really liked me and wanted me to marry his son. I said I wasn't going to marry him, but I decided to make him a pullover with three bicycles on it.

In early March, the final word came that we were to leave for America. They sent papers for all three of us. After that, we had to wait because there wasn't any transportation. Magda was staying in Sweden to be with Arne. Kis Magda decided to go home to Budapest, Hungary.

So, Manci, Edith and I filled our rucksacks with all our worldly possessions, which included some clothes and food. Then with our visas and boarding passes in hand, the Red Cross came to escort us to a steamship in Gothenburg.

The Drottningholm had been used as a diplomatic ship during the war. They had redone it for passengers, and it was quite luxurious. They were still working on it when we sailed. Most of the passengers on board were Swedish citizens and diplomats. There weren't very many refugees like us.

We had very good tickets; we even had our own cabin! It was a very rough trip at sea, though. There were violent storms and the ship was tossed and turned. Edith and I were sick the whole time. Manci kept telling us that we had to just forget about it. And then she got sick, too.

Of course, it was a Swedish ship and had wonderful smorgasbord, but as soon as I came into the dining room to eat, I had to run out to be sick. We traveled for 13 days, and for the entire 13 days I was sick

The ship made a series of stops as it approached the American coast. And as we came into the New York harbor, we saw the Statue of Liberty. Finally, we weren't alone anymore. The date was April 8, 1946.

PART 6

THE PHILADELPHIA STORY
1946-1948

Perhaps 50 million people were displaced because of World War II. A number of different refugee and relief efforts occurred before, during and after the war. The United Nations Relief and Rehabilitation Administration (UNRRA) was founded in 1943 and included the United States and 44 other nations. Its purpose was to "plan, coordinate, administer or arrange for the administration of measures for the relief of victims of war." It worked with dozens of charitable organizations to distribute four billion dollars in basic necessities. UNRRA also played a major role in helping displaced persons return to their home countries in 1945-46. It was later replaced by the Marshall Plan.

The US had a mixed record in response to the flood of refugees. In the late 1930s, the US received in excess of 100,000 applications from Germany and Austria, but maintained its strict national immigration quotas of 27,000. Immigration restrictions actually tightened as the refugee crisis worsened, largely due to antisemitism in the US government and because of a perceived fear that Jewish immigrants from Nazi-controlled territories could threaten national security as spies.

In general, US policy during the war in Europe was to not divert any military resources toward rescue efforts. However, by the end of 1942 the US government had adequate evidence to conclude that a campaign to annihilate the Jews of Europe was underway. While media accounts finally began to show the extent of the genocide taking place, public pressure remained somewhat muted until the Secretary of State, Henry Morgenthau, used his staff's report, *Personal Report to the Secretary on the Acquiescence of this Government in the Murder of the Jews*, to confront others in the US administration.

In January 1944, President Roosevelt issued an executive order to create the War Refugee Board (WRB). It was responsible for carrying out a new US policy for the rescue and relief of Jews and other minorities persecuted by Nazi Germany and its collaborators. The WRB organized secret rescue operations and channeled relief funds to various private groups and governmental agencies, especially in Scandinavia. The WRB launched a propaganda campaign to warn perpetrators that they could face legal punishments after the war and negotiated with neutral countries to allow more refugees to cross their borders.

Katie and Harry

March-December 1946 — Manci

I was determined from day one to start a new life. And we were so fortunate, so lucky, to start that new life with Aunt Katie and Uncle Harry.

Aunt Katie was my mother's half-sister and she looked like my grandmother who had lived with us in Munkacs. My grandmother died in the ghetto before we were sent Auschwitz. Aunt Katie had come to America when she was fairly young. But she and my mother were very close and sent letters back and forth all the time before the war. She had met Harry in America. Harry was from a poor village near Munkacs and was an unassuming guy, but with natural intelligence.

They had two boys and a girl: Willy, Bernie and Molly. Willy was married to Goldie and Bernie's wife was named Henrietta. Molly, the youngest, was married to Martin. Harry had a General Motors wholesale parts business. He used to get up early every morning and go to the store, and then he would call home to see how Katie was doing.

They had a big house on 4th Street in Philadelphia. Molly and Martin were still living there, but they gave Ipi, Edith and me the whole top floor of the house. They were the best and treated us, including Edith, like we were their own children. Harry was a *mensch*. The kindest person you would ever meet. He used to play the numbers, so whenever he won, he would slip me five dollars and say, "Don't tell anybody." But I knew he did the same with the other girls, too.

After a while, I started working for a friend of the family, a dentist named Dr. Korman. He was Goldie's dentist, so it was really her who got me the job. He had a practice that was in the suburbs — Oxford Circle. The hours were from noon until nine o'clock at night because he just saw people from his neighborhood. I was taught to do hygienist work for him and I got to be pretty good at it. He paid me peanuts. I nonetheless thought I was rich.

Then my uncle's bookkeeper, who had worked for ages at his business, got pregnant. So, I went to work for him and even got a raise, too. It was 30 dollars a week, which was a fortune to me.

My mother had a brother in the US, too. Uncle Herman was my mother's youngest brother and had managed to come to America right at the beginning of the war. He left without his family, hoping they would follow, but they did not make it out of the camps.

Uncle Herman was determined that we would become "Americanized." On his own, really, he had adapted our names on the naturalization papers. Ipi's given name was Regina Rella. No one ever called her Regina. She usually went by Rella, and I stuck to Ipi. Uncle Herman gave Ipi the name Ruth: Ruth Rella Grunberger. She liked it. Soon she became Ruthie. To this day, everyone calls her Ruthie. Edith was really Edit in Hungarian, so hers didn't change much.

Then there was me. Uncle Herman gave me the name Mildred. I hated it, so I kept using Manci and compromised with my official name as M. Manci Beran.

Long, Quiet Nights

March-December 1946 — Ruthie

I remember that Uncle Herman and our cousin Willy met us in New York when we arrived. We had papers already, so we came right off the ship with only our suitcases. We didn't bring many clothes, but the Red Cross in Sweden had given us Kotex, so we filled our suitcases with them. We didn't expect people to open our suitcases when we arrived; Manci and I were so embarrassed.

As the first days and weeks passed, we became more comfortable with our new home and even put on weight. We laughed that now we had to watch what we ate; otherwise, we would become too fat.

We had many long, quiet talks at night with our aunt and uncle, describing everything we had been through. They asked many questions about our last moments with Mother and Father. They listened with great empathy, and when there were times, we did not feel like talking, they patiently waited until we were ready again.

Since we were among the first Jewish refugees to immigrate to America, our names became sensationalized in the local papers, and curious neighbors started coming by the dozens to see us. There were also many relatives of people who had been in concentration camps looking for information about their families. Finally, my aunt and uncle stopped them from contacting us. It was just too much for us.

Even though our days were usually quiet, nights were often difficult for me. I continued to have nightmares for months after our arrival as I relived the last few years in my mind.

In spite of the pain and awful memories, some normalcy in our lives had returned. I enjoyed my first Passover in America with Aunt Katie and Uncle Harry. I delighted in helping my aunt clean the house and get ready for the holiday. Part of my job was to prepare everything for the Seder plate, like boiling eggs and roasting a shank bone in the oven while I was thinking about the many things Mother had taught me. I also helped prepare the *maror* and the *charoises,* just like Father performed these tasks. Although my aunt kept a kosher house, they would travel and do things on Shabbos. They were more modern than my parents, maybe more Americanized.

I began working. At first it was at a shoe company, putting the edging tape material around the shoes. I hated it. Edith got a job in a lampshade factory. Then a new friend helped me get a job at the same electrical supplies store where she worked. I worked in the office on an addressograph machine and even worked half days on Saturdays.

We knew that our uncle Sigmund — Father's brother and Edith's father — had survived the war. Years later, following a long time of correspondence and after wading through tons of paperwork and red tape, we were finally able to bring him to America.

The reunion with Edith was very emotional.

Uncle Harry and Aunt Katie in Philadelphia (date unknown).

Edith, Manci, and Ruth in Philadelphia (1947).

Manci in Philadelphia (June 13, 1947)

Manci and Kurt Beran's wedding photograph
(September 1948)

Ruth in Philadelphia (August 1947).

Ruth and Ernest Mermelstein (February 1948).

A Young Man from Vienna

1947-1948 — Manci

I met Ruthie Goldstein not too long after coming to Philadelphia. Her parents were from Germany and she took me under her wing. She was maybe a little older than me and tried hard to help us assimilate by taking us to youth clubs and the USO.

Ruthie and her parents lived very close to Aunt Katie and Uncle Harry's home. I would see her often before Ruthie moved. I was working nights as a hygienist and I didn't get to see the Goldstein's new house. So, Ruthie called me one night very upset because I didn't come to see her. My sister and Edith were doing something else, so I decided to come and see her.

There were a group of people present. One was a young man named Kurt. Ruthie had met him at the USO and he had stopped by that night to return an umbrella. I thought maybe he was her boyfriend and I kept saying to myself, "Gosh, I wish he would get a haircut." When I was ready to leave, he was leaving, too. He asked if he could call me and I made some stupid excuse. The next day I checked with Ruthie whether she was dating him and she said they were just friends from the social clubs. So, when he called, I said yes, and we started dating.

Kurt was Austrian and had been living in Vienna when his father died. He was four years old. His mother died six months later. He also had a brother who died at a young age. His aunt, Margaret, tried to adopt him after she got married to Julius Baar, but the law in Austria didn't allow women of child-bearing age to adopt. Because of that, he was never adopted, but essentially became their son.

Kurt's family was Jewish. When Hitler came to power, an uncle in Panama was able to get them temporary visas, and all three of them went there when he was 11 years old. Then the US wanted to clear Panama during the war, and they were allowed to come to America. They wound up in Philadelphia, on Chestnut Street.

He tried to enlist in the army when he was 17, so Margaret and Julius had to sign for him. He was sent to the Philippines. He had gone into intelligence and then later right after the war he was working as a civilian in Japan when I was coming to America. When we met, he had returned and worked at Dupont and was waiting to enroll in college at Temple University.

I will never forget one of our first dates. Years ago in Munkacs, I had read *The Wind Blew It Away* in Hungarian. I was so excited when I found out it had been turned into a movie: *Gone with the Wind*. Although Kurt had already seen it he took me to see it. The theater was packed, so we stood for two and a half hours. I came home and said, "You know this guy stood with me for two and a half hours," and my cousin Molly said, "Oh, it must be serious!"

Eventually we talked about getting married. Ruthie had met someone, too. She wanted us to have a double wedding. Of course, I was the older sister so I was supposed to get married first, but I didn't care about that. Kurt was in school and we had decided to wait. Ruthie got married in February. We were married the following September at my aunt and uncle's home. I wore an aqua dress with maroon accessories. I kept coming down and up the stairs greeting people. My Uncle Herman was furious at me because I wasn't hiding like I was supposed to. But I wasn't hiding anymore.

A Baker from Gorond

1947-1948 — Ruthie

I met Ernest Mermelstein more than a year after coming to America. He was from Gorond, Czechoslovakia, which was very close to Strabichovo where my grandparents had their farm and Ansci and Manci has been born. He was the eldest of six children of Ethel and Abraham Mermelstein. Four of the Mermelstein children, Ernest, Eugene, Sol and Clara, along with their mother, survived the horrors of the Holocaust.

It was not for lack of trying to leave that the Mermelstein family remained behind in Europe. In the late 1930s, they saw the dangers and made arrangements to immigrate to America. By 1940, all of their paperwork was in order, and it was decided that Abraham, the father, would go first, find a job and get settled. Then he would send for the rest of the family. But he soon received the devastating news that no more ships from Europe were being allowed to sail to America; his entire family was trapped in Czechoslovakia. Most of them ended up in Auschwitz. Ernest worked at a bakery in Budapest and was taken to forced labor, *munka tabor*. He ultimately went to Mauthausen and Gunskirchen. At the time of his liberation, he had typhoid fever but managed to recover. Ultimately, the family survivors were reunited with Abraham Mermelstein in America.

Ernest was visiting relatives in Camden, New Jersey and stopped by my uncle's house to visit. It turned out we had a great deal in common. I already knew his mother and sister because my maternal grandmother had lived very close to his hometown in Czechoslovakia. We used to visit my grandparents during our summer vacations, and I remember the Mermelsteins with great fondness. Moreover, Ernest had suffered terribly during the war, and he and I could relate to and empathize with each other's experiences.

Every Saturday we went sightseeing. One day, we went to the zoo and he just said that maybe I should marry him. I said yes and that was it. We were married on February 1, 1948, ten months after we met. The wedding was at a hall in a synagogue. It wasn't big, just the immediate family. I wore the white wedding dress of my sister-in-law. Manci was my maid of honor and Kurt was Ernest's best man. We went to Atlantic City for our honeymoon.

I was still working at the time. When I left the company, they filled a table of electrical products for me as wedding gifts. They gave me an iron and a pressure cooker which, by the way, I still have.

Manci married Kurt in September, and then a few years later our cousin Edith got married to Izzy, who was born and raised in Philadelphia. He was going to Drexel University and wanted to become an electrical engineer. They had a lavish wedding at a big synagogue hall.

All three of us had finally found a new home and new families.

PART 7

LIVES LIVED
1949-

In addition to the many important individual accounts of Holocaust survival that have been written over the past 75 years, there have studies based upon oral histories and memoirs as well as research that compared Jewish survivors with groups of Jews who had not experienced the trauma of the Nazi concentration camps. While generalizations are necessarily difficult in this kind of research, there are some broad traits that distinguish Holocaust survivors who managed to build successful lives from those who were undone by wartime trauma.

A study by Françoise Ouzan (2018) reveals three types of redemptive narratives that shaped the reconstruction of Holocaust survivors' self-identity. First, there is a social narrative that highlights their occupational and social achievements. Next, an ideological narrative that represents the homeland of Israel as a vital refuge for Jews facing antisemitism. And finally, there is a religious narrative that expresses preoccupation with the continuity of faith. The crucial role of "belonging" also emerged as being critical to part of their rehabilitation, for instance to organizations of survivors, to the new host country or to Judaism as a culture. Another common factor shared by those who successfully rebuilt their lives is "hyperactivity." The same determination that helped individuals survive also helped them engage in constant activity aimed at proving to themselves and society that they were useful.

A comprehensive, seminal study by William Helmreich (1992) suggests that many survivors of the Holocaust tend to be more successful than other American Jews of comparable ages. They had more stable marriages, often married to other survivors, and a lesser need to seek psychiatric help. Survivors exhibited a virtual absence of criminality. They tend to be particularly concerned about their children and are overprotective parents. While some benefited from their ability to share their wartime experience with others, there were others who used positive adaptation to seal off part of their emotions and memories.

Evidence from this research suggests ten general traits in survivors who were able to lead positive lives: flexibility, assertiveness, tenacity, optimism, intelligence, distancing ability, group consciousness, processing the knowledge that they survived, finding meaning in one's life and courage.

A Degree and a Commission

1948-1952 — Manci

I continued to work at my uncle's business. We didn't have much money, so Kurt and I got a rundown apartment on Randolph Street, right off Girard Avenue. Frici, who was still in Montreal, would come down to see her brothers in Harrisburg and then stay with us. The apartment was really only one room, so she would sleep in a big "crawl-in" closet.

We would often go up to New York on the weekends by car to see Ruthie and Ernest. You couldn't really get cars at the time, but Uncle

Harry had a connection in the auto industry. It was a Studebaker and we even drove to Montreal several times to see Frici.

We also spent a lot of time at Katie and Harry's home. They loved Kurt. He was Jewish, but had never been observant. Still, he also respected their home, as did I. I would never have done anything to hurt them in any way — of course, they weren't as strict as my parents had been. They even worked on Saturdays and Katie and Molly didn't cover their heads by wearing wigs even though Orthodox women often do not show their hair in public after their wedding.

Kurt had started back at Temple University on the G.I. Bill. He found out he could get paid extra for joining the Reserve Officer Training Corps (ROTC) and he seemed to like it. In order to be certified in ROTC he had to go to summer camp when he was finishing his degree at Temple. He graduated at the end of the summer camp as "The Distinguished Military Student." That gave him the chance to compete for the regular army at a time when the military was shrinking.

I was totally against him joining the Army at first. In Europe, the only people who went into the army were the very rich or the bums, so it was very difficult for me. Ruthie and I had our dark experiences with the military, too. She was concerned, but she was always great about live-and-let-live. She was very clear that it was our choice. My aunt and uncle, however, were very patriotic. None of their kids were ever in the army, so they tried to talk to me about supporting his idea.

Kurt went through a competitive process working in different areas and then the top students got a choice. He really liked the idea of seeing if he could do it, to prove to himself that he could be successful. Again, it was a difficult choice but finally we agreed. He spent a year at different locations around the country. At the end, he was one of the top students and was offered a commission as a 2nd Lieutenant. He chose transportation and logistics. I stayed in

Philadelphia during that time in our little apartment on Randolph Street.

There were so many new experiences. I remember that this was really the first time I had seen Black people other than in the movies. It bothered me when I heard people — mostly other refugees and Jews — refer to them as *schwarz*. It was said with such disdain. I used to say, "How can you do that when people called you Dirty Jew?" Auschwitz had made me very tolerant.

When Kurt graduated from his summer ROTC program, his company commander was a Black. He was one of the nicest people you could imagine. The Officer's Club in the army was segregated. I got a call one evening from Kurt that he wanted me to meet him at the Latin Quarter in New York. He said they were going to give the commander a farewell party and they couldn't do it at the Officer's Club. I was furious.

I guess this was about the time when Ruthie and I had our only problem. I was done trying to please everyone. She would ask on various issues, "What would our parents say?" And I would reply, "I wish they could say anything, but they cannot." They were no longer here. And since I could not live their lives, I wanted to live my own life.

Flatbush

1948-1952 — Ruthie

I moved with Ernest to Williamsburg, New York, into a big, three-bedroom apartment on Vernon Avenue. In the beginning we had two boarders: my father-in-law's cousins, Jackie and Herschel.

We wanted children, and soon we had a girl, Evelyn. As soon as she was able to sit, I sat her on a toilet. Within a year she was trained.

Ernest was still working at a bakery in Brooklyn where he used to work at night and would be home during the day. There was a big park close to where we lived — Tompkins Park. Many European refugees lived in the area and would bring their children in carriages to the park. At the time, it was tough. Nobody had any money. I had Evy and we would meet friends there. Ernest would often come after work and bring everybody Pumpernickel bread. They really appreciated it and kept telling me what a good man he was.

After a few years we were told we had to move because they were going to make our apartment building into a church. I had always been used to having a house, and so I told Ernest we needed to look for one, and we found one on East 18th Street in Flatbush. We had 1,500 dollars in the bank and needed to put down 5,000 dollars. Jackie, who had a very good job and was single, lent us money, as did my in-laws, as well as Kurt and Manci. It was a two-family house. We lived downstairs while Ernest's brother and his wife lived upstairs.

At some point, my two brothers-in-law, who had learned about upholstery in Munkacs, opened a furniture store together with Ernest. They were in business for a while, selling living room sets: couches and chairs.

And then there was my sister-in-law's husband who had learned watchmaking in Munkacs. He opened a business and asked my younger brother-in-law to be his partner. And then Ernest joined, too. In the beginning, Ernest's office was a trunk. He traveled all over, as far as Albany. Then he opened a booth on 47th Street in Manhattan where he sold watches, and I was the bookkeeper.

By that time, in 1951, I was pregnant with our son, David. Manci was in Virginia then and came to visit and help. She didn't have any children, so she and Kurt took Evy with them back to Virginia. I was a week or so late with David, so Manci kept Evy with her for two weeks.

An Officer's Wife

1953-1957 — Manci

I became an army wife. But we agreed that he would serve the minimum amount of time, which was 18 or 20 years, instead of what would be a full career of 30 years. The transportation corps headquarters were in Newport News, Virginia, so we began every assignment from there.

Our first assignment was brief. It was only a year or so in El Paso, Texas. What made El Paso special was that it was the place I gave birth to my first little girl, Rhonda Margaret. We went back and forth between naming her Veronica or Rhonda because Kurt was set on calling her "Rhonnie." Her middle name was after Kurt's aunt Margaret, who had raised him after his parents died.

The very next year, 1954, we were assigned to Germany. My family was anxious because they thought it would bring back all the bad memories. Uncle Harry and Aunt Katie were very concerned, and Ruthie was really anxious about it. My thinking was that this was a new life. I was going there as a US-military officer's wife and that was it. He was a first lieutenant then and was made captain when we were there.

Rhonnie was very small. Kurt met us at the airport when we flew to Germany with his driver and she screamed and screamed because she had never seen him in uniform. When he tried to hug her, she was screaming bloody murder.

When we first got to where he was stationed in Germany, there was no housing on the base in Vaihingen, so Kurt rented a small, older apartment. It was right above a bar, but close to the base. I didn't tell the neighbors that I understood German. They would very freely speak in front of me about the stupid Americans. I told Kurt, but said don't you dare tell Uncle Harry because he would send me a ticket to come home.

We didn't have a car because we had arranged for our car to be shipped before they went on strike. I was stuck in the apartment and was going nuts. One of Kurt's friends felt sorry for us and would come on the weekends and drive us around. Once he drove us to another city close by where I saw a big fat German guy with a beer in his hand in front of an apartment and I just started crying. How come he got to live in a nice place while I was living in a hole? That was the only time I lost it. Kurt and I decided we'd better move.

They were building a whole new base for the helicopter squadron not too far from the headquarters where Kurt was working, where they had an excess of apartments. It was a fantastic apartment, with three bedrooms and a maid's quarters on the third floor. We moved to Esslingen after six months.

One of Kurt's sergeants got married, and we were at the wedding. We came home and the maid, Elvira, looked sort of cute. She said, "I have a surprise for you. Someone is here to visit you." She opened the door, and there were Magda and Arne! It was so amazing. We really thought we would never see each other again. And yet there they were. Magda and I had been talking over the telephone, and she knew where we were living in Germany. When we had left Sweden, she had been very emotional and kept saying, "I'll never see you again."

They actually came about four times to see us, each time unannounced. Once they came when we were supposed to go to the general's house. I called up the general and said we had unexpected guests. The general said to bring them along. Afterward, we all went bowling — all dressed and everything. Arne and Kurt got along very well right from the beginning.

Shabbos Goy

1953-1960 — Ruthie

I think the house next door in Flatbush was owned by a Greek couple. They had no children. When they both died, the house went up for auction, so we bought it. It was a one-family house, which we tore down and had it built into a three-family house, and moved downstairs into one of the units.

In Sweden, Edith, Manci and I didn't eat kosher. We ate everything. In Philadelphia, we followed the example set by Uncle Harry and Aunt Katie. Harry never wore a hat, for example, and he worked on Saturdays. Aunt Katie kept a kosher home, but they weren't that strict, so we acted the way they did.

Ernest wasn't that religious either. We went out on Saturdays after we got married. We talked on the telephone, too, which isn't something most Orthodox Jews do. But Ernest's family was Orthodox. My in-laws were exactly the same as they were in Europe. My father-in-law, Abraham Mermelstein, was already here and my mother-in-law, Ethel, had survived the camp and had come here with four of their children — Eugene, Sol, Clara and, of course, Ernest.

Manci was with us one Saturday, Shabbos, in Flatbush. We were going somewhere. She waved at someone we knew who was walking on the street. I remember saying, "Why did you do that?" I said it because we were in a car and Orthodox believed you should be commemorating that G-d created the world in six days and so the Torah commands us to rest and not to work on Shabbos.

My sister-in-law lived upstairs and would never even eat in my house, because I wasn't strictly Orthodox. It wasn't good enough for her. My mother-in-law wouldn't eat in my house either.

When I had my daughter, I sent her to Hebrew school, because the elementary school in our area wasn't very good, and education was better in the Hebrew school. Evy had a friend from school in the house one day on Shabbos when the phone rang. I picked it up and spoke, which one is not supposed to do on Shabbos. The girl called me "Shabbos Goy", that is, acting like a non-Jew. I felt that I had embarrassed my daughter. After that I made a deal with myself: If I am going to send her to Hebrew school, then I have to do things like they teach it. I shouldn't act two different ways. I would eventually have to take her to a psychiatrist because she wouldn't know which way was right.

My daughter really changed my life. Ernest was okay with it. If I hadn't met him and his family, I would probably be the way I was before — maybe not like Manci, but rather religious, but not strict, just like I was raised in Munkacs and how Uncle Harry and Aunt Katie were.

After camp a lot of people stopped believing in anything. Maybe that was what happened to Manci or maybe she was always that way even before what we went through. I don't know, but it was her life to live in this new country with Kurt.

Making Memories, Removing Memories
1953-1957 — Manci

I was excited about the possibilities of travel. We got to be very friendly with other people in our apartment building during Kurt's post in Germany. One was a colonel and his wife, the Taylors, and we traveled with them to Vienna and Paris. We also took trips to Switzerland, Belgium and the French Riviera.

We also visited Sweden which was very emotional for me. Magda and I didn't talk very much about camp. Like me, she wanted to live her life and wasn't religious either. When she went to Auschwitz, it was as a resistance member. Only later did they find out she was Jewish.

Magda and Arne had a lot to do with my decision to have my tattoo removed. Magda had already had it done. They said once you decide you want a new life then you don't want a tattoo because you don't want to be a martyr. People would feel sorry for you. In the army, others were aware of my past. I didn't lie about it. Kurt had "no religious preference" on both of our papers, but he didn't like me being subjected to questioning about the war and Auschwitz.

We talked about it with Uncle Harry, Aunt Katie and Ruthie. What would they think? I wasn't that keen on having physical memories. I knew I would always have my memories, no matter what. I asked Arne, who was a doctor, removed the tattoo. For a while I had quite a scar, but as time went on it faded. I was never sorry that I did it. I wrote to my aunt and uncle telling them that I had it done. They wanted me to forget; anything I did to erase the memory was okay with them. Ruthie was more open about her past and was always willing to tell her story. At the same time, she never held it against me that I didn't want to dwell on my past. She was so sweet; that was just who she was.

In the winter of 1956, I had a second girl: Sandra Kay. Kurt just really liked the name Sandy. By then, we had been in Germany for three years and we were going back to the States. Magda and Arne had three daughters and the last time they came to visit was, as usual, unannounced. They were going to Spain. But we had made extensive plans to go to Venice. By the time they left, we went directly to Italy. We got there late but ended up at a very fancy hotel. It was a fantastic trip, and the last one we took before leaving Europe.

It had been more than ten years since we had been taken from my home in Munkacs with my entire family and sent to Auschwitz where they had been murdered. Since then, I had been anxious about pleasing everyone all the time. I think Ruthie felt that the army changed me. But in the army, I didn't have to pretend. The army actually liberated me.

Camp Winsoki

1962-1966 — Ruthie

I was at Camp Winsoki for three or four years. It was a summer camp for boys and girls located upstate, near Albany, on a beautiful lake. The parents were mostly very rich. Since they were traveling for the summer, they sent their children to camp. We sent Evy and David there one year, after which the owner asked me to be camp mother for the girls. I stayed all summer.

I used to wash their hair and watch them when they were swimming. I would put towels on them so they wouldn't catch cold. I would go say goodnight to them in their bunks. I was like a mother to them. When little kids were homesick, I would help them and empathize with them about missing their families.

Ernest would come up for weekends, bringing up fresh lox and bagel from New York. He would help out and returned home for work on Monday. He couldn't just sit and do nothing, so he tried to help. Not that he was asked to, he simply offered. Ernest would even help with the laundry.

We became good friends with the owner. After the first year, she gave me a beautiful coat rack as a gift so that I would come back. They didn't pay me much money, but I was very happy because otherwise I would have stayed home all summer doing nothing. And this way I was with both of my children.

The parents were raving about me because they never had such a good camp mother. I was embarrassed. And the parents used to give me tips. I felt ashamed. They were very, very nice to me and made me feel that I was helping their families, too.

In 1966 I got pregnant again and had a little boy, Howard. Years after having David, I had a miscarriage in my fifth month. Evy was very upset when that happened. She locked herself in her room; she really had been waiting for this baby. Evy had wanted a sister because of how close I was with my sister, her Aunt Manci. I told her not to worry, and that I would have another one. And then I did, but it was a boy. Howard (we called him Zvi) was 14 years younger than David.

After Zvi was born I gave my first speech. It would have been in one of Evy's or David's classes. A teacher asked me to talk about the Holocaust. I didn't know if I could do it but I just felt that someone had to do it, when asked.

The students asked me about my tattoo. When my kids were little, they saw it and would question me about it. I used to tell them that I always forgot my phone number, so I put it on my arm. In the classes, however, I would say, "I am not ashamed of the number. Whoever put it there should be ashamed."

They also said they were surprised I didn't cry when I spoke. I told them I had learned to cry on the inside.

School Days

1957-1964 — Manci

I knew that coming home from Europe, we would initially go to Newport News, Virginia, because that is where his unit's home base was. But where? We had very good friends — he and Kurt had parallel careers — who had just gone back home to the US. They bought a house in a new development and we decided to join them there. They actually bought our house for us; in fact, we never saw it. It was a little ranch house with a big yard and a carport.

During the three years of our stay there, we got to see Ruthie and Ernest and their kids a lot. Rhonnie was about David's age, while Sandy was still a toddler. Frici, my dearest friend from Munkacs, and her husband, Steve, had moved to Harrisburg and they had two children about the same age, so we were always visiting each other.

Then we were stationed at Fort Levenworth, Kansas for a year during which Kurt went to the Commander General's Staff College. We went back to Philadelphia right after Kansas because Kurt had been accepted into the MBA program at the Wharton School of the University of Pennsylvania. Since the army was paying for it, they really pushed him hard and he graduated in one year and a semester. We had a big house in Alden, outside Philadelphia.

His next assignment was a hardship tour in Korea without family. He knew all the professors at Temple University, and since Kurt was afraid that I would go nuts, he arranged for me to take any course I wanted. Rhonnie was ten and Sandy was seven or eight, so I took the courses when the kids were in school. The three of us moved to an apartment where Kurt visited a few times, surprising the kids.

I would go and take the train. Because I had a business background in Europe, I picked similar kind of subjects. Uncle Harry and Aunt Katie's youngest son, Bernie, had two sons — Stevie and Barry — who were in some of my classes. I accumulated a lot of credits and got all A's.

I loved it. I could have spent 24 hours a day at school. I wasn't going for a degree. Rather, I just wanted to sharpen up my accounting in case I ever got a chance to work at it. I remember one professor with whom I argued about one of my exams. He wanted to give me a B. I kept asking him why. Finally, he said, "Let's settle on A-." I was so independent. I had very good professors and had their full cooperation. They knew I wasn't trying to get a degree. It was just so much fun to learn.

With Kurt in Korea, Ruthie and Ernest would come down and we would meet at Uncle Harry and Aunt Katie's house. We were very close during that time. I would pack up the kids and drive to Harrisburg to spend time with Frici and Steve, too.

I was a good army wife. There were a lot of restrictions I didn't like such as the fact that my kids weren't supposed to play with sergeants' children. That bothered the hell out of me, but I didn't want to have any negative influence on Kurt's career.

In Germany I was on all these committees. As treasurer, I had to listen to this stupid general's wife, and when she tried to give me orders, I was not happy, but I didn't say anything or create any problems. Kurt used to come home for lunch, and he would see me go to the medicine cabinet for an aspirin or something and he would say, "Oh, you had a meeting, didn't you?" But I never did anything to jeopardize his career.

Ruthie and I are very different in that respect. She was so accommodating, so nice. I was never that way. I was the different one and, to be honest, I wanted to be different. I don't like to be hemmed in or be told what to do and how to do it. That was why school — the freedom to think — was so important to me.

Ernest and Ruth in Brooklyn (1955).

Manci and Kurt, Baden-Baden Germany (1956).

Ruth and Ernest with Evy (1949).

Kurt with Rhonnie and Sandy in Nellingen (1956)

Ruth and Ernest with Evy and David (1956).

Kurt at 7th US Army Headquarters, Frankfurt (1956).

Ernest, Ruth, David, Evy and little Zvi (1966).

Manci and Kurt in Honolulu, Hawaii (1965).

The Israeli Connection

1968-1975 — Ruthie

I remember that when we were in Sweden, there was a lot of pressure on us to move to Israel. Eli, who was in charge of us at Fjallgarden, really wanted us to go there. He kept saying that they needed us. But Manci didn't really like it. Maybe it was because our parents had been against the Zionists before the war. Or maybe after what we had been through, Manci just wanted us to be somewhere safe.

Ernest and I had followed events taking place in Israel after we got married and had children. We knew people who had moved there. After the war in 1967, we decided to finally go to Israel ourselves and stayed with my childhood friend, Zahava.

Around then, Evy was graduating from high school and had been taught Hebrew language and culture and the Bible by Israeli teachers. After her graduation, she decided to spend a summer on a kibbutz in Israel before going to Columbia University. On another trip, in the summer of 1968, she volunteered at a hospital in Jerusalem and met Shalom Orkaby, an Israeli boy, at the movies in the Sinai Peninsula. He had been a paratrooper before in the army. He said he was going to stay in touch with her when she returned to the US to finish school at Columbia.

Anyway, she got a package from Shalom, containing a red beret and paratrooper wings. Evy said, "He must be a very nice boy because he kept his promise." Evy visited Israel in December 1969, and in September 1970 Shalom moved to the US. He was working as a security man for El Al. When they told us they wanted to get married, we really didn't like it at first. My in-laws were against him, simply because they didn't know him or his family — they were Arab Jews from Yemen. We wrote a letter to my cousin's brother-in-law who lived in Israel, to find out about the family. He later said to us, "If he is Yemenite, and he is religious, you don't have to look for anybody better."

Evy and Shalom were married in the summer of 1971, with Rhonda, Manci's daughter, as a bridesmaid. When in 1973 there was another war in Israel, he went back to fight. Our son Zvi was a little boy and he would look at the TV to see if he could see Shalom because he missed him so much. Everybody at the shul cried when he left, and it was such a happy occasion when he came back after the war. They had a daughter, Yael, and Shalom started going to Baruch College and studied to be a CPA.

In January 1979, they moved to Israel where Evy started to work as a pharmacist, and Shalom with a large accounting company. They bought an apartment in Rishon LeZion, but returned to the US 15 months later where they had another daughter, Adi. They still have the apartment in Israel, though. At first, they rented a place about four blocks away from us. They looked all over to buy a house, and couldn't find anything. We found out that the people across the street from us wanted to sell. Evy and Shalom looked at it and bought it.

Shalom's friends told him not to move so close to his in-laws but he and Ernest ended up being best friends; they were inseparable. Every Sunday, they would go to Borough Park to go shopping, then they'd have lunch afterward and come home and sit on the steps together. They loved each other.

Aloha and Aloha

1964-1969 — Manci

I thought Kurt was going to be assigned to the consulate in Hong Kong after Korea. He would have been an attaché, and we would have joined him there. Due to a Hungarian uprising at the time, they thought it would be a political risk. Because Korea was considered a hardship tour, they allowed him to choose his next assignment. We chose Hawaii. It was so enjoyable for us and the kids. The military had a beach on Waikiki — Fort DeRussy Beach — and we would go almost every weekend. They had two floating docks out in the ocean with diving boards.

There was one time in Hawaii where my past became an issue. Rhonnie was being a teenager, acting out. And Kurt wanted to make sure she knew how wonderful her life was compared to mine at her age. I had never told the kids anything. But Kurt would, at times, try to make them feel guilty. He would say they needed to be careful around me because I had been in camp.

I always felt I could handle it. I wasn't a martyr and I never wanted that. So, I made him stop doing that. We never talked about it again.

We had so many guests — long-lost coworkers, relatives and even two doctor friends of Arne from Denmark. Ernest and Ruthie visited us in Hawaii. Magda's daughter, Nette, even came from Sweden and stayed with us for several months. Once, Kurt and I took a wonderful trip with the kids to Japan and saw all the sights, including Mount Fuji.

Rather than flying back to Virginia after being stationed in Hawaii, we decided to make an adventure out of it. We sailed back to Los Angeles on the Lurline, a luxury cruise ship. We then flew to Toledo, Ohio and picked up an Oldsmobile 98, and drove it to Virginia.

It was 1968. Kurt had always said 20 years in the army; that would be it. But when the 20-year period was over, Kurt wanted to stay because he was up for promotion to full colonel. I kept saying, "There is always going to be a reason to stay." He was 42 years old.

Finally, I said no. I didn't particularly like the kids not having a home, and by then they were teenagers and they had friends. When they were younger, it didn't matter so much. And there was the possibility that his next assignment would be Vietnam.

I had a very good ally, his commanding officer at Fort Eustis. He was in Vietnam and he found it horrible. The GIs did all the work while the officers sat in their clubs and such. He was up for general. Since his wife was very sick, he had to return home from Vietnam. He kept saying that Kurt was too smart for that. According to him, you can get out after 20 years, and a little earlier if you have a good excuse. Also, Kurt only had to do 18 years because he was given credit for two years as an enlisted man during the war in Vietnam.

When Kurt was at Wharton, he had met Harold Strom, a visiting professor from the University of Oregon who had told Kurt that if he ever wanted to get a PhD, they had a great program there.

It was the middle of the school year. Rhonnie and Sandy had just spent three years in Hawaii when Kurt received his orders back to Newport News, Virginia. We then made the decision for him to retire instead, and so our last army move was to Eugene, Oregon.

German Soil

1979 — Ruthie

I guess Ernest and I had caught a little bit of the Zionist bug, especially after the war in 1967, and so we visited Israel. Right after Evy and Shalom had moved there, we decided to go visit them for Passover. After we booked the flight, we were told that El Al had gone on strike which meant we had to transfer to another plane, a charter. Because the new crew had been on duty for so long, they had to divert to another airport and wait for a different crew. The stopover was Frankfurt, Germany.

I couldn't understand people who, after the war, were able to go back to Germany and live there. For me, to set foot on German soil was terrible. We had to wait. Jewish passengers were really upset and were yelling about being stuck for hours in Germany. Ernest and I had Zvi with us, who was around 11 or 12 at the time. It was a confusing and exhausting experience.

When we finally got to Israel, the captain announced that we had to stay on the plane because the stairway was broken. It ended up being a 25-hour trip from New York. We were very, very tired. When we were going to leave after the visit, El Al said they'd heard about our trip and if we wanted to stay a few more days, that would be okay. I said, "No, I want to go home already."

But we missed them and so later that same year we made plans to go back for High Holy Days and *Sukkot*. The apartment where they lived didn't have any Orthodox families. We even built a *sukka*, a temporary hut, as part of the celebration.

When it came to the last day of the holiday, *Simchat Torah*, there was a festivity in Rishon LeZion that involved dancing around the Torah in a big park. We had already been there once, and Ernest had met some people at the synagogue. One of them went to the mayor who was conducting the dance, and said, "We actually have somebody from America over here and it would be nice if you called him up to be one of the dancers." So, the mayor announced it on the loudspeaker: "Would Naphtali from America please come up and help with the dancing?" That made Ernest's day.

I think Manci and Kurt went to Israel once; it was part of a sightseeing cruise with Trans World America (TWA). They spent time with Hendu, but I don't think my sister had the same pull I felt to Israel. Maybe it's being more comfortable with the new country versus the old country, or maybe it's because of the greater focus on religious practices throughout the Israel culture, but Manci and Kurt don't define themselves as Jewish in that way. Or maybe she just doesn't want to be reminded of our past.

I am very supportive of Israel, but never actually wanted to live there. There was too much conflict and hate between people and countries in that area. I've seen enough of that, so I am content to go visit.

A Working Woman

1969-1983 — Manci

I went to work for Jim Callahan in 1969. It was just him and a CPA and me. Callahan treated me as an equal. It was heaven on earth; he was a wonderful boss. He had been an army brat and would always accommodate my needs for anything. Eventually he decided to expand. He brought in two CPAs who I couldn't stand, because they treated me like an underling. The CPA who was the original partner felt the same way. He told Callahan he wanted to leave and open his own office. And then he came to me because he knew I was very unhappy. He asked me to come with him and I said yes. Callahan tried to talk me out of it, but I just said I didn't like the atmosphere. That was it. He wanted to give me a farewell party, but I said no thank you; I just wanted to go. One day, it was pouring rain, and there he was at my house with a little jewelry box and a necklace with a tennis racket on it, accompanied by a beautiful personal note.

I worked for Callahan for ten years and then another five years for the other CPA. Callahan wrote a wonderful recommendation letter which I still have. It says, "Mrs. Manci Beran has been employed by this firm for almost ten years. During that time, she has been an exemplary member of our staff. She was very loyal, hard-working and most conscientious. She was well liked by all clients with whom she came in contact. We regret Manci's departure, but understand and sympathize with her reasons. We would welcome her return any time."

Kurt started teaching at the University of Oregon almost as soon as we arrived from Virginia. He received his doctorate in 1974 and was offered a professorship at Oregon State University in Corvallis, 40 miles away. He commuted with another professor from Eugene.

By then, Rhonda had gone to Southern Oregon College and had transferred to the University of Oregon after her freshman year. Sandy was already attending Oregon State University. She spent her four years there and sometimes would go by Kurt's office to have lunch.

Kurt and I continued our traveling. In 1974 we went to Mexico and from there flew on to Costa Rica. Kurt said that since we were this close by, we should visit Panama, too, where he had first lived after leaving Austria before the war.

In 1977, we traveled to Rome, Capri and Sorrento. We also went to Israel where I got to see my cousin Hendu again. She had been liberated by the Russians and had gone back to Munkacs, married a local guy and got a government job as a law clerk. When the Russians allowed Jews to emigrate in the 1960s, they moved to Israel.

We went to Alaska the following year. We took the inland passageway from Vancouver. And a few years after that, we went on a cruise in the Caribbean, from Nassau in the Bahamas through the Virgin Islands.

Whenever we traveled, we went first class. We just never denied ourselves anything, including cruises and vacations. And every time we took a trip, we would buy a postcard and put it on a large bulletin board. The bulletin board is absolutely full, and to this day hangs in my garage. We went back to Hawaii, too. Ruthie and Ernest met us there. I am pretty sure Edith and Izzy did, too. We would stay at the military hotel, called Hale Koa.

I think Frici and her husband Steve may have come to Hawaii as well. Frici and I saw each other whenever we had a chance throughout the years. But if not, we talked on the phone or wrote. We were that close. Always.

Returning Home

1989 — Ruthie

I had always wanted to go home again, to Mukacevo, Czechoslovakia, which had become Munkacs under Hungarian rule. The area had been occupied by Russia after the war and ultimately became Mukachevo in Ukraine. Ernest also wanted to go, and we took along our daughter, Evy, to show our roots.

We flew into Budapest, where we hired a taxi driver who drove us to Strabichovo, which was still part of Hungary. I wanted to find my grandmother's grave because Evy was named after her. Although it took some time, we eventually found it. The headstone was barely legible. The neighbors came to see us and see who we were. They brought us a scrubbing brush and Evy kept scrubbing until we could clearly see the name on the stone.

Because we had some friends still living there, we were able to order a new monument. In addition to the names of my grandmother and an uncle, we also put on the monument the names of my parents and three sisters and three brothers who had been murdered in Auschwitz. They never had graves.

We then crossed the border into Ukraine in order to visit Munkacs. I had always dreamed of finding my mother's engagement ring and wedding band that she had buried in the front yard of our home to safeguard them from the Germans.

From the hotel in Budapest, I took the largest spoon that I could find to dig in the garden. Our house was still there, but it had been converted into three apartments. One of the people invited us into his section where our kitchen had become his bedroom. Another person living there actually thought we had come to take the house back. I told him, "I don't want the house back because I have a much nicer one in America." The area in the front — where my mother had her garden — had been cemented over. I told the person who thought we were taking the home back that my parents had buried gold coins there. (She hadn't. Just the two rings.) The next year, when we came back, it was all dug up!

We went in the following years, too. One year, my husband and I returned to *kever avos* to see the new monument. We also visited the grave of the Munkacser Rebbe. Another year, we found the grave of my grandfather who had died in hospital in the nearby town of Beregszasz.

While it was heartbreaking to see all the places that I had known as a child, I still felt it was important to go. All the streets that I remembered as being so big and grand seemed small and dingy. Everything was old and dilapidated, and yet I could still see things as they once were.

Spanish Literature

1983-1989 — Manci

I was happy that 1983 began with two weddings. Both of our daughters were married that year: one in January and the other in March.

After graduating from the University of Oregon, Rhonda was working in the office of the Business School. There, she met Daniel, a graduate student in the PhD program. They started dating, and Rhonda earned her MBA while he was finishing his doctorate.

They were married at the Officer's Club at the Presidio, a military base in San Francisco, where Rhonda was working for a bank. It was a small, non-religious wedding because neither of them were religious. Ruthie and Ernest, of course, came and were so happy for Rhonda. A cousin, of mine, Anshu, who I thought was a terrific guy and who I was pretty close with, was invited, but told me he wouldn't come because Daniel wasn't Jewish. Apparently, Anshu just wasn't that accepting.

After graduating from college, Sandy had gone on vacation in Europe where she had met a young man on a train in France. Tracy was a Canadian and his family was from Vancouver. They had a long-distance relationship for years. Instead of getting married at a non-religious setting like Rhonda and Daniel, they were married in a church in Portland, Oregon, where she had been living and teaching. No one from our side of the family attended other than us and Rhonda. To me, religion causes so many problems. Everybody thinks their god is the only true god. I guess when you are religious, you are lucky because your religion gives you all the answers and you can just follow a set of rules. But how could God have allowed Auschwitz?

Once we settled in Oregon, I started taking classes during the time the kids were in school. I was just doing it for fun. Kurt and I used to go to school together. I was always a part-time student, taking classes all over the place. I took Physics, my favorite class, Chemistry and History. Other than an Economics class I didn't take anything that had to do with business. I had amassed quite a few classes over the years. I was taking Spanish courses, too. I was jealous that Kurt spoke a Latin language, and despite all the languages I spoke, I could never quite understand what they said when traveling throughout Europe.

One day, the dean called me in and said that I was accumulating too many credits. "You have to decide on a major," he said. We looked at the number of units I had and decided on Spanish Literature. All the remaining classes were given in native tongue. I remember how tough Don Quixote was in Spanish and needed a dictionary the whole time.

I graduated in 1989, magna cum laude, and I was made a member of Phi Beta Kappa, the national honorary society. My college degree is on the wall in my home, right next to my 1944 class picture from the Royal Hungarian Business Academy.

I didn't go to graduation, though. Kurt's birthday was right around graduation time, and we had a tradition to drive to Reno to gamble. You could make it in a seven-hour drive from Eugene. Before we went, I borrowed a gown and Kurt took a picture of me dressed up in the dining room and then we went to Reno. The new MGM had just opened.

The Miracle Man

1990 — Ruthie

I woke up feeling awful. We had just returned from a trip to Munkacs and Israel. At first, I thought it was merely a jet lag, but soon I was vomiting with awful headaches. I went to the Emergency Room and then was admitted to Columbia Presbyterian Hospital, where they took CAT scans and an angiogram. I was diagnosed with a hemorrhage on the right side of my head and an aneurysm on the left side. I needed surgery.

Manci flew in at once, arriving the night before my surgery. The doctor said, "We'll open your head from ear to ear and take care of both sides at the same time." He made it sound like it was a simple procedure, and I guess I was glad he was so confident.

When I think back, I see this incident as one of the many miracles that occurred during my life. I had a hemorrhage in my brain for 11 days before the surgery. The procedure itself lasted eight hours. It is amazing how the hand of G-d is present in all things. In order for the aneurysm not to rupture, I needed to develop a hemorrhage, which in essence saved my life. Weeks after surgery, I had double vision and so my surgeon recommended I see an ophthalmologist. My appointment was August 13, 1990.

On that day, Ernest and I started the two-hour drive late in the morning. I was looking down at the tape deck in the car and pushing buttons. Suddenly, the road felt bumpy. Ernest had fallen asleep and when I looked up, we were speeding down an incline heading straight toward water. The car plunged into a lake and slowly began to submerge. As the water rapidly began filling the car, I became hysterical because Ernest couldn't swim. Then I noticed that I had torn the stitches in my head and was bleeding profusely. I was sure that we were going to drown. I struggled to open the doors, and eventually the rear passenger door miraculously opened. I swam out and got to the shore. It was rocky and there was a fence I had to climb over. Somehow, I made it back to the road and flagged down a car. A woman stopped to help me but later I learned that a truck driver had seen us veer off the highway and had radioed the police. Even before they could get there, two men had stopped. One man had pulled Ernest from our car and the other had administered CPR.

Ernest was not expected to live through the night due to severe injuries. David's wife, Nina, got to the hospital first, and then Evy and Zvi arrived. Zvi's wife, Tova, came with Shalom that evening. David was at a conference in Dallas and flew back home on the first flight. So many people supported us when we needed them: Manci and Kurt, our grandchildren said *Tehillim* every day in their schools, and many people were praying at the *Kotel* in Israel.

I had suffered three cracked ribs and needed 31 stiches on my forehead and another 22 to repair the ones from surgery. Ernest was in and out of a coma for a week and on a respirator. He was intubated and fed through a maze of tubes for many more weeks. At one point he was shocked back to life. He lost 39 pounds and spent seven weeks in the Intensive Care Unit. Over the next few months, he went from a wheelchair to a walker and then to a cane. He never fully recovered, though. His heart was permanently weakened, and the tracheotomy left him hoarse. But he had made it — the hospital nurses named him "the miracle man"!

At two pivotal times in our life, the *chevra kaddisha* was on standby: during the Holocaust, and years later, at the time of Ernest's accident.

Sentimental Journey

1988-1991 — Manci

I was married to Kurt Beran in 1948, so the year 1988 was important to us. We had been so fortunate in our lives, so lucky to have found each other, to have had children, and were leading successful and fulfilling lives.

At the beginning of that year, Sandy and Tracy treated us to a wonderful trip. We flew to Vancouver, Canada. We then took a train through the Canadian Rockies and Jasper National Park, from Vancouver to Lake Louise, Banff and Edmonton. It was so incredibly beautiful.

Then we went on what Kurt called "our sentimental journey." We were away for more than a month, starting in Copenhagen, and from there we took a train to Vienna. We had briefly been in Vienna when we had been stationed in Germany, but this was really my first time experiencing the city where Kurt was born. Next, we went to Budapest, where Hendu and I had gone on a mission for Father just before Germany invaded Hungary. We stayed at the Hotel Intercontinental.

In Budapest we went to a restaurant where they had a gypsy orchestra play for the guests. The conductor went from table to table and asked if people had a favorite song they wanted to hear. I told him I had a favorite song of my mother and father. But I said, "You wouldn't know it. It was a long time ago." The song is about an avenue of acacias in Budapest. It starts, "When I go, I remember..." Anyway, he knew it! *Akacos Ut.* What a treat! It was also so much fun being in a country where Kurt couldn't speak the language. Everywhere else we went he was fluent, whether it was German, Spanish or Italian.

I also looked up my dear friend Kis Magda who had returned to Hungary after Sweden. We had kept in touch throughout the years. Hungary was in dire economics for a long time, though, so I used to send her things, such as fabrics for a dress. We went out to dinner with her and her husband. They later took us on a boat trip down the Danube.

Then we went by train and ferry to Dubrovnik in Yugoslavia and flew back to Copenhagen. A few days later we went to Sweden to spend time with Magda and Arne.

We had done so much traveling in the military that this was sort of natural to us. And besides, we loved to travel, especially by this time. The kids were married and we were on our own. We had the money and we always wanted to see and experience new things.

I know Ruthie was different that way. She and Ernest had their regular routine consisting of Munkacs and Israel, mostly. She knows Israel inside out. For them, going to Israel was like me going to downtown Portland. Kurt and I just liked going to new places and having experiences rather than dwelling on how things were.

Ruthie and Ernest also went to Desert Hot Springs in California in January and February each year. They had a motel apartment with cooking facilities and would bring their kosher cookware and utensils from Brooklyn. There was a synagogue nearby. Kurt and I would drive down every year from Eugene and stay for at least a week. Rhonda and Daniel joined us a few times because they were living in Los Angeles by then. Even Sandy and Tracy would fly down from Vancouver with the kids to visit.

Manci worked as a bookkeeper in Eugene, Oregon (1970).

Ruth and Evy at grandmother's grave in Strabichovo, Hungary (1989).

Manci and Kurt on Royal Viking cruise (1999).

Ruthie and Ernest at Aschi's Bar Mitzvah at Western Wall (1997).

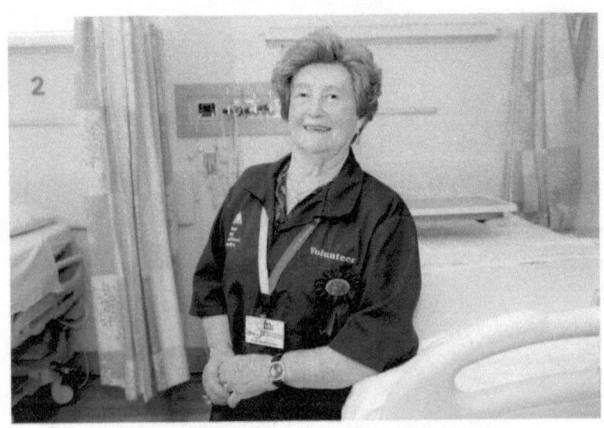

Ruth volunteering at Mt. Sinai Hospital (2018).

Sandy, Manci, Kurt and Rhonda (2016)

Return to Auschwitz

1997-1998 — Ruthie

I was so privileged to donate a *Sefer Torah* to a shul in Brooklyn in 1997. For Ernest and me, the *Hachnasas Sefer Torah* was one of the most special days in our lives. We dedicated the Torah in memory of our parents' *z'l*. *Hashem* had been so good to us and we wanted to demonstrate our gratitude. We felt that this was the most fitting memorial to our dear parents, who had lived Torah-true lives. In turn, we had taught our children to be Torah-observant Jews. *Baruch Hashem*, the legacy lives on in our children and grandchildren.

The next year, 1998, was our 50th-wedding anniversary. Ernest and I planned a special trip with our children and grandchildren consisting of 16 people in total. We first went to Budapest, as we had always done. We stayed at the Beke Hotel, in room 238, just like we had done since we first went back in 1989 with Evy. The staff always reserved the same room for us.

We had a bus and a bus driver, but I remember that we took along our taxi driver, too. We had hired him when we made our first trip back to Munkacs. His name was Istevan, and he became a very good friend. He knew all the places we wanted to go, so we didn't have to explain things to the bus driver.

What made this trip different — other than taking 16 family members with us — was that we continued our travels into Poland. Ernest and I had decided that we wanted to show my family members what I had gone through. We decided to go back to Auschwitz.

We took the standard tour. A tour guide showed us two bunk beds. and commented that eight people had had to sleep in one bed. I went over to him and said, "That's not really true. There were 12 or 13 in one bed."

There were also two younger couples from America, who were originally from Poland. Their parents must have been real antisemites because they said they came to find out if maybe Jews deserved what they got. So, she came over to me and asked me, "What did you do to deserve this?" I responded, "It was just because we were Jewish." She apparently wasn't satisfied, so she asked, "But maybe you did something?" I finally said, "Listen, I had a four-month-old baby sister. What did she do?" She started crying. We saw her near the road later on, and she was still crying.

The only place I didn't go to was the crematorium. I saw it from across the street, but I couldn't go there. I sat on a bench babysitting Hillel, my first great-grandchild. He was such a good boy.

How could I have gone back to Auschwitz? Many might wonder about that. I am the strong one. Manci was the strong one in camp, while we were going through it. But after that, I was determined to face it, to talk about it. That's why I do the speeches. Whenever someone asks me, I cannot say no because somebody has to. So I keep telling the story. For others it is simply history, but it is different for me.

On the Golf Course

1997-1999 — Manci

I think at some point the rain in Eugene began to get to us. Kurt was about to retire from his second career as a university professor, and we started to consider other places. The first place we looked at was Palm Springs. Ruthie and Ernest had been coming to the area for many years, and we would drive down from rainy Eugene to visit them. One year, we decided to have a real estate agent take us around. We found one house that was beautiful with air conditioning even in the garage. We were ready to make a deposit, but the guy had to find the papers or something, so we needed to come back the next day. And when we got to the motel, Kurt said that he really didn't like it because it was a Del Webb type of project and you could see other houses. We started to do our homework. We always came in January and February when Ruthie and Ernest were there. In that season, the weather was beautiful, but we actually didn't realize how horribly hot it could get in the summers.

The next year we were meeting Sandy and Rhonda for Christmas, and we decided to meet them in San Diego. Just before leaving home, we received our annual home insurance policy through the military. It contained a notice that if you were moving, they had a service where they would contact a realtor to make the process easier. Since we were going to San Diego anyway, we decided to have them arrange for someone to show us around.

The realtor asked us what we were interested in, such as what price range we were thinking of, what size of property, and so on. Finally, she said, "You want Rancho Bernardo." The real estate person ended up meeting us at the plane and took us around. At first, Kurt found something wrong with everything. Then we went back again when Rhonda moved to Los Angeles. This time the agent took us to this new development. Kurt fell in love with the place, but there wasn't anything available. It took a year and a half until a house became available. Kurt, most importantly, wanted something on the golf course. He didn't play golf but he just wanted the openness, the view.

After we settled in — maybe within a year or two — we took a big vacation. It was a Royal Viking Cruise through the Mediterranean. We really loved Royal Viking Cruises, and we had taken one cruise ten years earlier through Baja California in Mexico, Puerto Vallarta, Acapulco and down to the Panama Canal.

A few years later we went on my dream trip. We flew to Hawaii then sailed to New Zealand and on to Australia and Tasmania. It was the "best of the best." After that, I came home and said, "That's it. I am finished traveling." But Kurt announced that after I had my New Zealand vacation, he wanted to have his dream Mediterranean vacation, too. We decided to do that as well. That cruise was magnificent: Barcelona, Malta, Egypt, Athens and the Greek Islands. A lot more postcards were added to our bulletin board!

We always felt we had done things the right way. Kurt had worked hard and had had two full and successful careers. I had worked, too, putting money away in an IRA every year. We had no mortgage. The kids were doing well and didn't need our help. We didn't have extravagant taste by any means, but on the other hand we also didn't deny ourselves anything. We were both determined to live life to the fullest.

Beyond the Tracks

1998 — Ruthie

I had gone to see *Schindler's List*. Everyone around me cried. I didn't shed a tear. To me, it was like looking at it from the outside. Manci had the same reaction. You almost asked yourself, "Did that happen to me?"

Steven Spielberg used some of the revenue from the movie to form the Shoah Foundation, which was dedicated to making audio-visual interviews with survivors of the Holocaust. In September 1995, they came to my house in Flatbush. There was an audio/video person and an interviewer, Leslie Bennett-Troper. The interview was a few hours long. I did it because I had to do it, and I wanted to do it. They gave me several copies of the tapes. I gave one to Edith and she said, "Why did you say your name is Ruth? We used to call you Ipi."

I vowed that if I ever got out of that living hell, I would tell people what we went through. That's why I wrote the book as well. I think I must have started writing right after the Shoah interview. I did it at home, by hand. I went back through my diary, my *naplo*, from Sweden. The diary was written in Hungarian and it was a lot longer than I remembered: 27 pages.

It was difficult to begin writing. I covered my life growing up in a loving family in Munkacs and wrote about our misery after being swept up and sent to Auschwitz, and then discussed our months-long march into Germany. I spoke about our Grunberger family history, as well as Ernest's family history. I decided to include the horrible tragedy of our accident from six or seven years earlier. It was a difficult process. I was writing one day and Ernest was upstairs sleeping. When he came down and saw me crying, he said, "Stop it. I don't want you to do it." I said, "No. I have to do it."

My granddaughter, Yael, helped me with the writing. It was difficult for her, too. Many of the events are difficult for a stranger to read, let alone a relative. But I could not have finished it without her.

We went to several publishers and were rejected for various reasons. Eventually, I gave a copy to a friend of one of my children. He was very impressed and went to the Orthodox Union that accepted my work for publication and gave me an editor to work with. *Beyond the Tracks: An Inspirational Story of Faith and Courage* was published in 1997. Rabbi Moshe Krupka of the Orthodox Union said in the

Foreword, "The Orthodox Union is pleased to publish this touching and heroic memoir. We are indebted to Mrs. Mermelstein for sharing her most personal memories. We appreciate how difficult it must have been. We are confident that those who read this book will be fortified with the *emunah*, *bitachon*, and *avodas Hashem* which the pages contain."

They offered me a royalty for the book, but I told them to donate it to charity. I didn't want to make a penny on it. They sold 5,000 or 6,000 copies in the first ten months, and then the second printing came out a year later. I added a glossary because not only Jewish people read it, and I added some text since I had visited Beregszasz that year and had found my grandfather's grave.

Wherever I go to speak, I take along a copy of my book and donate it to the school or library. I vowed I would write a book, and I did. It took me a long while to become the person I became.

Mental Exercise

1999-2009 — Manci

I loved to play bridge, and so did Kurt. When we first moved to Rancho Bernardo, we became friends with a fellow who lived just outside our gated community. His name was Jake and he ran a bridge game with lots of people and teams. The club was really strong. Jake's wife, Alice, got very ill and he asked Kurt to substitute for him. When Alice died, Jake didn't want to continue and so Kurt ended up doing it for 12 years.

It is a fantastic mental exercise. Of all the cards and hands I've played, I honestly don't remember ever having the same two hands. It was always great socially, but I loved the mental part even more.

Kurt and I even followed professional players in the newspaper. We used to play at the Officer's Club. Kurt and I always played as a team and we were good. You have to be competitive, and we were. But it's more a question of being competitive yourself rather than actually winning. Ruthie is more complacent, not competitive. She is so easygoing. But she is also very true to her beliefs. So strong. That's why everyone likes her. I am more decisive. I'm more of a take-charge person. That's why in camp, Ruthie was more willing to let me decide things.

We also always loved old movies, the classics. Kurt literally could tell you the Academy Award winners of each year from the 1940s to the 1970s — Lauren Bacall, Spencer Tracy, Bette Davis and all their movies and Alfred Hitchcock movies, too. He would ask me to tape movies on DVDs even though he would have seen them a million times before. Rhonda and Sandy also used to give us those classic movie compilations for birthdays or Christmas.

Kurt was always fascinated by history and by World War II movies and books. I just considered all Nazi movies very shallow. I think Kurt sometimes felt guilty that I went through all that and he escaped the trauma. I just didn't ever want to talk to him about it, but if he asked a question, I would answer it.

I remember when we watched *Schindler's List* in the movie theater everyone was crying, whereas I kept thinking, "You think that was bad?!" When Ruthie and I talked about it, I found out that she had the same reaction. I don't think she cried either because it was just a movie to us. She said people don't realize that the movie doesn't represent anything close we went through. It wasn't that it was inaccurate, but she was looking at it as a stranger would. I agree. I also looked at it from the outside. I still cannot picture myself doing those things or going through all of that. I couldn't have done it.

A Long Brief Goodbye

2005-2009 — Ruthie

I call it my new old house. When we were first married, we bought our house in Flatbush. Then we built a new house next door and moved into one of the upper-floor apartments. We lived there for 30 years. After Ernest had his accident, it was hard with all the steps, so we moved back to the bottom floor of our original house. That is how it became our new old house.

At some point, we had two women helping with Ernest. One was Maureen, a wonderful Jamaican woman who was so good to Ernest. I recommended her to other people, too. She became part of the family and even calls me Mommy. Unfortunately, Maureen had surgery at some point and couldn't come back. She has a daughter and granddaughter who live with her now. We still stay in touch. I usually get her a little gift on her birthday, which is June 12.

With Maureen gone, we needed another helper for Ernest, and so we had Zura, who was from Georgia, the country. He lived with us and had his own room. He was very, very good.

Both Maureen and Zura were great. I sort of adopted both of them, really. They became part of our family and could not have been better people and friends.

After Ernest had the accident, he never felt good and wasn't himself, but he was okay until the last three or four years of his life. We always had someone accompany him. He used to say, "Please G-d take me already." Being a real workaholic, this was no life for him. I have a whole wall in the dining room filled with pictures of the kids and the grandkids. I would take him to the dining room and say, "Look at this. Look what you have to live for."

In January 2009, we had gone to Desert Hot Springs, like we did every year, when Ernest got very sick. He was diagnosed with acute leukemia and died within a few days. Zura was with us at the time.

Nina, David and Zvi flew in from New York and Florida. Ernest saw them for a last time and talked to them. That was good. Before he died, he said, "I don't want to die" which broke my heart, because since the accident he had always been asking to go, and now he said that, right before he died.

The Jewish Burial Society, Chevra Kadisha, came and picked up the body and then he was brought to New York for the funeral. It happened the next day, as is Jewish custom.

In 1989, Ernest and I had first gone back to Munkacs. I don't think we missed a year for the next 20 years. After he died, I never returned. I have continued to go to the Palm Springs area in January each year. My children come and visit me there, but mainly I get to spend time with Manci, who lives only two hours away. And I continue to speak whenever I am asked. I have to. I had a friend who worked in a school in Palm Springs and the children were learning about the Holocaust. They were wonderful and hugged me. I gave them a book for the library. The school has asked me back several times. I cannot say no.

Looking Forward

2009-2013 — Manci

I know one of things that appealed to us about being in southern California — other than the weather — was access to a military base. The Marine Corps Air Base at Miramar was only 20 minutes away. We often went to the commissary there to shop. We also took a lot of walks together in our little neighborhood. Because it was gated, there was never a lot of traffic. The other thing we would do is go to the public library in Rancho Bernardo to get books.

Rhonda and Sandy had given me a machine. It wasn't a fax or a computer, but it allowed me to receive emails and pictures. It was called a Presto. I now had an email address! That was great and before too long I was getting emails from everyone. My grandkids — Lauren, Cameron and Emma — were always sending me things. When I had trouble with it, Rhonda tried to explain it to me. She is a real technology whiz.

Then one Mother's Day, maybe 2013, they got me an iPad. I was a little afraid at first, but I had become pretty good with programming the new TVs, and I had adapted from VHS tapes to DVDs to DVRs, and then to the new models. With the iPad, I could send and receive emails and text messages. Frici loved the fact that we could talk to each other that way. Seeing all the pictures from everyone is so much fun. I watch some of the news on TV, but I now read most of the news on my iPad. Sandy and Rhonda send me emails during the day and links to stories, mostly about the crazy political environment we have been in. They do it all day long.

Ruthie and I talk every day now. But she doesn't have any interest in computers or things like that. I send emails to Evy who lives next door. She prints them out and shares these with Ruthie. I think I am like Rhonda. I have a sort of natural need to try to understand things. I want to know what each button does. I have my own signature now for text messages. I figured out the characters: emojis.

Maybe I am more forward looking and Ruthie is more interested in tradition and the past. I remember that years ago, Izzy wanted to read my diary from Sweden. I don't know why. So, he asked me if he could have it. I had never translated it into English. I don't think I had ever looked at it. Anyway, I gave it to him. When I got it back, he gave me the original and a copy in English that said, "Translated by Edith (Grunberger) Milner." Even then, I just put it away. I didn't want anything to do with it.

I do think that, if possible, Ruthie and I became even closer after Ernest died. I mean, we were always so close. We weren't, of course, when we were at home in Munkacs. She was younger and mother would always want me to take her with me everywhere. But I had Frici and she had her friends, like Edith. That all changed in camp. We would not have survived without each other. That is still true.

The Waldorf Astoria

2009-2016 — Ruthie

I always wanted to be a nurse, but life had something else in store for me. When my husband passed away, I wanted to do something. Both Ernest and I had been patients at Beth Israel Hospital in Brooklyn, and I decided to volunteer there.

Ernest died in January and I started work in September. I go to see the patients after they give me a list. I take the papers and magazines. I say, "Hello, I am a volunteer. I came to see how you are feeling. Feel any better? Can I get you anything?" And a lot of times they ask for something. Maybe ice water, or another magazine, or a tea or coffee.

Sometimes I help people eat by cutting up their food. There was a woman who was almost blind. When I came at lunchtime her tray was in front of her. She wasn't eating. I asked why she wasn't eating. She said she couldn't find the silverware. So, I helped by feeding her. I recently had a woman crying. I had to sit with her for 15 minutes and spoke to her, after which she quieted down. Another example, there was a young guy whom I asked, "Could I get you anything?" He said, "Your smile made my day." I cannot be a nurse, but I like to help people.

The hospital is about half an hour walk from my house. I usually walk there and back. Sometimes, if the weather is bad, Evy will take me by car. Otherwise, I'll take the bus.

I became close friends with the volunteer coordinator. Maya lives in New Jersey, and a lot of times when she has to go in early the next day, she sleeps at the hospital. We are very close friends.

I received my first achievement award maybe eight years ago. The event was held at the Waldorf Astoria. It was in the newspaper. There was a picture of me, and on the other side a picture of my family. It was so nice. Now when they have volunteer awards, they sometimes ask me to speak. I am embarrassed because they introduce me as a writer and show everyone my book. Since then, they have given me nine awards. They have a shul at the hospital and I know the rabbi. When I received my ninth award, the rabbi was sitting next to me and said, "Well, when you get the next one, we can have a *Minyan* and start to pray." At synagogue you need ten men before you can start to pray.

In one of the recent hospital newsletters Maya said, "I can honestly say Mrs. Ruth Mermelstein is a grandmother to everyone in the Mt. Sinai Brooklyn community." Well, I have three children, 12 grandchildren, and now 48 great-grandchildren — so maybe it is true.

I was told that I am the only volunteer who is a Holocaust survivor. I just like to help.

Time Flew

2014-2018 — Manci

I knew that Frici always answered my emails, except the last time. After a few days, I just knew that something was very wrong. When I called her daughter Vivian answered. I found out that Frici had cancer but didn't want anyone outside the family to know. I was in shock and hung up because I didn't want to know.

I immediately called Ruthie and I was screaming. Ruthie said you need to call her back. Vivian said that her mom didn't recognize anybody at that point. But she gave her the phone anyway. I said "Frici" and she said "Manceeee!" She had a funny way of saying my name. So, I knew she recognized my voice. She died that day. It hit me so hard. I really fell apart. That was several years ago.

Rhonda and Daniel were visiting us when Kurt was not feeling well. We got him to the doctor's office that day; he was diagnosed with pneumonia and was admitted to hospital. His health declined after that, with heart and lung problems. We were hopeful, though, when he recovered enough to come home. We had a nurse and a physical therapist for him and had some railings installed for his safety.

Everyone was so wonderful. Ruthie came several times from New York to be with us. Sandy and Tracy and the kids kept coming from Canada, and Rhonda and Daniel would come down often, too. The neighbors in our little community were very kind.

After several months, Kurt was readmitted to hospital, and it was decided he would be moved to an adjacent nursing facility. I developed a routine over the next four months of going every morning and staying throughout the day. I would help feed him and try to make sure he was as comfortable as possible. They had a cafeteria, and I had my iPad to read the news and to keep everyone informed about Kurt.

One day, Rhonda was going back home and Sandy wasn't arriving until the next morning. Rhonda didn't want me to sleep alone, so I slept in Kurt's room for the first time. He died that night. I first called Rhonda who was on a train. I was very grateful to have been there, to be with him at the end. That was so important to me.

He was buried at Miramar National Cemetery. There was a full-honor guard and a rifle salute. The people there were so kind and treated him and me with such dignity and respect. I was proud of that.

If the war had not happened, I probably would have married someone who appealed to my parents — like one did back then — and I would have been unhappy. I feel guilty that I had to lose my parents, go to Auschwitz and come here to marry the man I would be happy with.

I was lying in bed last night and couldn't fall asleep. I was looking back at my life because it is coming to a fast end. I couldn't get over all the things that have happened in my life. When you start looking at it, you ask yourself, "Did that happen to me?", "Did I go through that?" I couldn't fall asleep. It was a horrible night because I had to face reality for the first time. It is a shame it has to end this way — first Frici and now Kurt. I don't see how I can get over this, how I am going to do it.

Ruthie stays longer now when she visits because we found out that Ralph's grocery store in La Jolla has kosher food. She now stays over Shabbos and we get her candles out. She calls every day at 7:00 p.m. to check up on me. She is worried about me, like I used to worry about her. She is a very, very, very good sister.

It seems like time just flew. But when you start thinking of the details, it is different. Today is April 8. It is the anniversary of when Ruthie, Edith and I arrived in the United States.

The Wall of Fame

2017-2018 — Ruthie

We have a charity box on the coffee table in the living room of my new old home in Flatbush. Several times a year, a man comes to pick it up. This spring, a younger guy came and saw that my wall was full of pictures. He remarked how nice it was. I said, "Yes, it is nice because I never thought I would have them." He asked why, so I told him. I then told him to come into the dining room where I have my "big" wall with all the pictures. I call it my "Wall of Fame." He asked if he could take a picture of it. He was so enthused. In fact, I had more to add and needed to start a new row at the top. Shalom helped me. That is my revenge — *nakooma*.

My children, grandchildren and great-grandchildren are my revenge. That's it. I never thought I would have any, so that is how I refer to them. And I tell you, that's what I live for. They are all wonderful children. Every Friday, every time the phone rings, they call to wish me a good Shabbos because Saturday is my day of rest.

I have a calendar with all the kids' birthdays on it. At the beginning of each month, I write cards and get cash from the bank for each one. Most of them live upstate in Monsey and so David's wife, Nina, gathers them all up and delivers them. She functions as my mail man.

Sometimes I go with Evy to the Museum of Jewish Heritage in Battery Park. A few years after she retired, she decided to volunteer there. She went through months and months of training. She said, "It was like getting a graduate degree in Holocaust Studies." It is a beautiful place. As a volunteer guide she takes groups of students around.

Years ago, I donated many of my pictures and items to a collection in Brooklyn. But then they opened a new museum — Museum of Jewish Heritage in Battery Park — and the collection was moved there. Not too long ago Daniel and I went and watched Evy gather the students on the tour around a picture of me when I was 17 years old, living in Sweden. Next to the picture is the hair comb that I made out of metal when we were marching through the mountains. Evy talks about it representing hope even under such horrible conditions. Finally, she told them that the girl in the picture was very special to her. Then she looked over at me and said, "Because that girl is my mother and she is here with us today." It was a very emotional moment. I am not just a picture. I am that girl. And then they started to ask me questions.

I go to Israel quite often, too. David's son, Shmuel, went to Israel after high school and liked it so much that he stayed. He got married and lives in Jerusalem now and runs a yeshiva for married couples. Adi, Evy's daughter, and her husband, Fred, moved to Israel years ago. They live in Ramat Beit Shemesh Aleph. She is a social worker and he is a CPA. They have six boys and a little girl. The basement in their house has two sides. On one side there is a room with a couch that opens. It is called "Bobbi's room," and that is where I stay when I visit.

I am very happy. But I still think about one thing: What did they do with my baby?

Ernest was in forced labor camps in Budapest working for the Hungarians. When the Germans came in, they killed most of them and sent him to Mauthausen. Ernest saw with his own eyes how the SS threw a baby up in the air and shoot it like a toy. Another Nazi told a mother to put a two-month-old baby on the ground upon which he stomped it to death with his boots.

If they had done that to little Peska, Mother would have died right there. So what did they do with my baby? It drives me crazy.

THE KITCHEN TABLE
JUNE 19, 2018

Manci and Ruthie

Manci: "I was just numb. Ruthie has a different tone. I was like somebody else looking in. It wasn't happening to me. To me, even now, I couldn't have gone through that. I am more detached. I know it happened. But I cannot believe it. It's too overwhelming because I could not have survived."

Ruthie: "I just felt all along that somebody had to do it."

Manci: "It happened to her. For me, it happened to someone else. It's in me and she lets it out. And probably she is better off."

Ruthie: "It isn't easy for me. I do it for the children."

Manci: "I couldn't stand up in front of a group and talk about it for anything. I couldn't even tell my own children about it. I couldn't. My diary in Sweden... I stopped after five pages because I couldn't handle it. I couldn't do it. I got that far and couldn't go on. I didn't ever want to talk about it again."

Ruthie: "I am the strong one."

Manci: "I was the strong one. Now Ruthie says she is. Maybe I was strong going through it and Ruthie is the strong one in dealing with it. I don't know. We did what we had to. We survived."

Ruth and Manci at the kitchen table in San Diego (2018).

EPILOGUE

Perhaps the most vexing question in doing research for this book was: Why were the sisters (and others) offered the choice to volunteer for a 'private transport' to Reichenbach in December 1944, which was then followed by an SS-guarded march to a series of other disparate work camps in Germany, and finally culminating north of Hamburg/Altona near the Denmark border?

We know their itinerary because Manci added a chronology in her short diary written in Sweden in 1945:

- May 21, 1944 - Arrived in Auschwitz
- May 24, 1944 - We were tattooed
- May 25, 1944 - We started working Birkenau
- December 15, 1944 - We volunteered for Reichenbach
- February 10 or 12, 1945 - We started to walk 25-30 kilometers a day through the mountains
- February 16, 1945 - We arrived in Trautenau
- February 16, 1945 - We were put into open cars and traveled for ten days
- February 26, 1945 - We arrived in Porta

- March 25-26, 1945 - Closed cars with 100 to 120 per car. We went to Bendorf, and after that to Ludwigslust
- April 15, 1945 - Hamburg - Altona
- April 30-May 1, 1945 - Our last SS-escorted transport
- May 2, 1945 - Arrived in Denmark
- May 4, 1945 - Arrived in Sweden.

These places have been identified and shown on the following map that describes the events after they volunteered for Reichenbach.

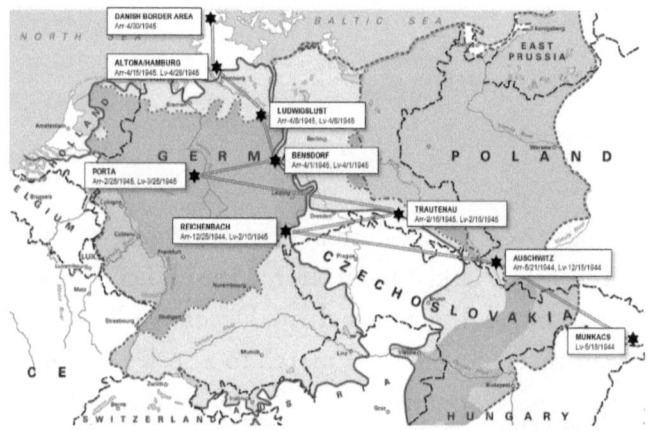

Manci and Ruth Grunberger's train from Munkacs, Hungary to Auschwitz, Poland (May 18, 1944 to May 21, 1944) and march from Auschwitz, Poland to the border of Denmark (December 15, 1944 to April 30, 1945).

Manci describes in early December 1944 that the guards asked for volunteers for a work detail. The person who was in charge was a civilian and it was called a "private transport." At that time, the Red Army was approaching, and the Nazis had begun preparations to evacuate concentration camp prisoners to the German interior. The major reasons for these actions were:

1. to not let prisoners fall into the Allied or Soviet forces and tell their stories,
2. to keep forced laborers to help maintain the war production, and, perhaps,
3. that some Nazi leaders were trying to use prisoners as hostages for peace negotiations.

Manci, Ruthie and others didn't know any of this. They just concluded, "We are never going to get out of here. There is no chance if we stay. We aren't really taking any chance if we decide to go." On December 15, the sisters were loaded on a cattle car for Reichenbach, for a ten-day journey.

The order to evacuate Auschwitz occurred on December 21, 1944 and the final evacuation began in earnest in mid-January 1945 in advance of the Red Army (and the Soviets entered Auschwitz on January 27). This practice was largely because the Nazis were determined to prevent the survivors from falling into the Allied hands. Many died by exposure to the severe weather or were killed by the SS when they fell behind due to exhaustion and starvation. Prisoners themselves and historians ultimately used the term "Death March" because the prisoners were marched under such extremely harsh conditions.

Many of the largest death marches were launched from Auschwitz and Gross-Rosen, and historical maps show the movements were to the west into the Germany interior. But the described "private transport" movement that Manci and Ruthie and the hundreds of other girls went northwest first, then back east, and finally to the north. They zig-zagged, unlike the transports that left from Auschwitz weeks later.

The most comprehensive analysis of these actions was conducted and published by Daniel Blatman in *The Death Marches: The Final Phase of Nazi Genocide* (2011). Correspondence with Professor Blatman at the Hebrew University in Jerusalem did not resolve this conundrum.

First, he said that being able to reconstruct a particular route was valuable and unique because, in many cases, "the archives are silent." Unfortunately, he wasn't able to shed any light on a clear and cut answer to the "Why" question because many events were influenced by "local developments and didn't come from an authoritarian entity in Berlin." And so, we are left with partial explanations.

Chapter 4 describes the different forced labor camps over the four-month trek. It should be noted again that the worse part was after the first camp at Reichenbach. That was a march on foot (20-30 kilometers a day) through the Sudeten Mountains back east to Trautenau in Czechoslovakia. Then there was a transport back west to Porta in the middle of Germany, and then again east to Bensdorf, followed by the transports north to Ludwigslust and then to Hamburg.

The final stretch was a transport north to the Danish border where the SS guards simply disappeared in an open field on the day Hitler committed suicide.

As the sisters have often said, the Nazis never shared information, they could only guess why they zig-zagged for almost five months and why their freedom ultimately came about so far north. Manci says, "What I didn't know then — and still don't know — is why we were spared. Were we just slave labor? At the time we were told that we were part of some deal. Supposedly, Sweden had been trying to exchange Jewish refugees for steel. Or was it a rescue mission conducted by the Swedish Red Cross?"

When Germany invaded Hungary in March 1944, Adolph Eichmann offered a deal where "one million" Hungarian Jews would be spared in exchange for certain goods, including 10,000 trucks. This deal was termed "blood for goods." The offer was not seriously considered by the Allies.

Other efforts were successful. Raoul Wallenberg, the Swedish special envoy in Budapest, was known to have saved thousands of Jews by issuing protective passports and sheltered Jews in buildings designated as Swedish territory. Count Folke Bernadotte of the Swedish Red Cross led what was known as the "white buses" expedition that transported thousands of Jews and women political prisoners from Ravensbrück and other concentration camps to Sweden for medical treatment and recuperation.

It shall never be known why the sisters were forced to march in such a seemingly haphazard way from Auschwitz to the border with Denmark. But the place where they were ultimately liberated was beneficial for them because they were quickly sent to rehabilitate in Sweden and then were in the US within a year. Most of those who were liberated in concentration camps in Germany, ended up in other refugee camps for several years. Some returned to their home countries and others were ultimately accepted by other countries, including the newly formed Israel.

The five girls were only a few days in Denmark and were then taken to Sweden by the Red Cross to recuperate. Within a year, Manci, Ruthie and Edith were among the first refugees that came to the United States.

SOURCES

Interviews

Manci Beran, August 9, 2017. Length: 1:50

Manci Beran, August 10, 2017. Length: 1:12

Manci Beran, September 4, 2017. Length: 1:22

Manci Beran and Ruth Mermelstein, September 15, 2017. Length: :32

Ruth Mermelstein, September 16, 2017. Length: :54

Manci Beran, October 11, 2017. Length: :47

Manci Beran, November 2, 2017. Length: 1:00

Manci Beran, November 3, 2017. Length: 1:31

Manci Beran and Ruth Mermelstein, January 15, 2018. Length: :25

Ruth Mermelstein, January 16, 2018. Length: 1:04

Manci Beran and Ruth Mermelstein, January 16, 2018: Length: :34

Manci Beran, March 18, 2018. Length: 1:23

Manci Beran and Ruth Mermelstein, June 19, 2018. Length: 1:24

Manci Beran and Ruth Mermelstein, June 20, 2018. Length: 1:30

Ruth Mermelstein, June 20, 2018. Length: :51

Manci Beran and Ruth Mermelstein, June 20, 2018. Length: :33

Manci Beran and Ruth Mermelstein, June 21, 2018. Length: :53

Other Primary Sources (direct use of language)

Manci Grunberger, *Journal of Recollections*, May, 1945. Translation by Edith Milner (May, 1996).

Rella Grunberger, *Diary*, May-June, 1945. Translation by Szilvia Gartner and Alexandra Major (July, 2018).

Ruth Mermelstein, *Beyond the Tracks: An Inspirational Story of Faith and Courage* (New York, Union of Orthodox Jewish Congregations of America), 1998.

Ruth Mermelstein Grunberger interview by Leslie Bennett-Troper for USC Shoah Foundation's Visual History Archive, September 19, 1995. https://sfi.usc.edu/

Section Sources

These two organizations provided comprehensive source materials for the historical section headings:

United State Holocaust Memorial Museum's Holocaust Encyclopedia https://www.ushmm.org/learn/holocaust-encyclopedia

Yad Vashem: The World Holocaust Remembrance Center

http://www.yadvashem.org

The following sources provided specific information.

Part I Never Wanting and Part II Growing Storm

Raz Segal, *Days of Ruin: The Jews of Munkacs During the Holocaust* (Jerusalem, Israel: Yad Vashem), 2013.

Raz Segal, *Genocide in the Carpathians: War, Social Breakdown, and Mass Violence, 1914-1945* (Stanford, CA: Stanford University Press), 2016.

Part III Descent into Darkness

Lawrence Rees, *Auschwitz: A New History* (New York, NY: Public Affairs), 2005.

Yad Vashem, The World Holocaust Remembrance Center, Central Database of Shoah Victim's Names https://yvng.yadvashem.org.

Part IV On the Run

Yehuda Bauer, *Jews for Sale? Nazi-Jewish Negotiations, 1933-1945* (New Haven, CT: Yale University Press), 1994.

Daniel Blatman, *The Death Marches: The Final Phase of Nazi Genocide* (Cambridge. MA: The Belknap Press of Harvard University Press), 2011.

Part V Paradise

Ralph Hewins, *Count Folke Bernadotte: His Life and Work* (Minneapolis, MN: T.S. Denison & Company), 1950.

Louise Borden, *His Name was Raoul Wallenberg* (New York, NY: Houghton Mifflin Company), 2012

Part VI The Philadelphia Story

Gerard Daniel Cohen, *In War's Wake: Europe's Displace Persons in the Postwar Order* (New York, NY: Oxford University Press), 2012.

Part VII Lives Lived

William B. Helmreich, *Against All Odds: Holocaust Survivors and the Successful Lives They Made in America* (New York, NY: Simon & Schuster), 1992.

Françoise S. Ouzan, *How Young Holocaust Survivors Rebuilt their Lives: France, the United States, and Israel* (Bloomington, IN: Indiana University Press), 2018.

ACKNOWLEDGMENTS

I wish to thank Rhonda, Manci's daughter and my wife, for encouraging me to take on this important work. She acted on many levels: motivator, fact-checker, and copy editor. Rhonda's sister, Sandy, was an early and formidable cheerleader. On the Mermelstein side of the family, I had the support of... well, everyone. But I need to thank especially Ruthie's daughter, Evy, who has been so kind to me personally and a steady source of enthusiasm from the very beginning.

I received a good deal of professional support as well. Connell Cowan, a noted psychologist, author and dear friend, coached me through numerous drafts of the manuscript. Raz Segal, who has written several books on the Jews of Munkacs and the Carpathians, was kind enough to give me feedback along the way.

I am also lucky enough to have a friend, Kelly Zuniga, who is the Executive Director of the Holocaust Museum Houston who helped connect me with Ann Millin, a historian at the United States Holocaust Memorial Museum (USHMM) who, in turn, connected me to other dedicated researchers and historians at the USHMM.

Rachel Beck, my literary agent from Liza Dawson Associates, has been an enthusiast promoter and friend to both me and the sisters from the very beginning.

And finally, to Manci and Ruthie, thank you for the great privilege of allowing me to tell your story of unconditional love.

ABOUT THE AUTHOR

Daniel Seymour is a tenured professor, administrator and consultant to many colleges and universities. He received his B.A. degree from Gettysburg College and his M.B.A and Ph.D. degrees from the University of Oregon. Dr. Seymour is the author of 18 books and lives in Palm Springs, California with his wife, Rhonda.

AMSTERDAM PUBLISHERS HOLOCAUST LIBRARY

The series **Holocaust Survivor Memoirs World War II** consists of the following autobiographies of survivors:

Outcry. Holocaust Memoirs, by Manny Steinberg

Hank Brodt Holocaust Memoirs. A Candle and a Promise, by Deborah Donnelly

The Dead Years. Holocaust Memoirs, by Joseph Schupack

Rescued from the Ashes. The Diary of Leokadia Schmidt, Survivor of the Warsaw Ghetto, by Leokadia Schmidt

My Lvov. Holocaust Memoir of a twelve-year-old Girl, by Janina Hescheles

Remembering Ravensbrück. From Holocaust to Healing, by Natalie Hess

Wolf. A Story of Hate, by Zeev Scheinwald with Ella Scheinwald

Save my Children. An Astonishing Tale of Survival and its Unlikely Hero, by Leon Kleiner with Edwin Stepp

Holocaust Memoirs of a Bergen-Belsen Survivor & Classmate of Anne Frank, by Nanette Blitz Konig

Defiant German - Defiant Jew. A Holocaust Memoir from inside the Third Reich, by Walter Leopold with Les Leopold

In a Land of Forest and Darkness. The Holocaust Story of two Jewish Partisans, by Sara Lustigman Omelinski

Holocaust Memories. Annihilation and Survival in Slovakia, by Paul Davidovits

From Auschwitz with Love. The Inspiring Memoir of Two Sisters' Survival, Devotion and Triumph Told by Manci Grunberger Beran & Ruth Grunberger Mermelstein, by Daniel Seymour

Remetz. Resistance Fighter and Survivor of the Warsaw Ghetto, by Jan Yohay Remetz

My March Through Hell. A Young Girl's Terrifying Journey to Survival, by Halina Kleiner with Edwin Stepp

---

The series **Holocaust Survivor True Stories WWII** consists of the following biographies:

Among the Reeds. The true story of how a family survived the Holocaust, by Tammy Bottner

A Holocaust Memoir of Love & Resilience. Mama's Survival from Lithuania to America, by Ettie Zilber

Living among the Dead. My Grandmother's Holocaust Survival Story of Love and Strength, by Adena Bernstein Astrowsky

Heart Songs. A Holocaust Memoir, by Barbara Gilford

Shoes of the Shoah. The Tomorrow of Yesterday, by Dorothy Pierce

Hidden in Berlin. A Holocaust Memoir, by Evelyn Joseph Grossman

Separated Together. The Incredible True WWII Story of Soulmates Stranded an Ocean Apart, by Kenneth P. Price, Ph.D.

The Man Across the River. The incredible story of one man's will to survive the Holocaust, by Zvi Wiesenfeld

If Anyone Calls, Tell Them I Died. A Memoir, by Emanuel (Manu) Rosen

The House on Thrömerstrasse. A Story of Rebirth and Renewal in the Wake of the Holocaust, by Ron Vincent

Dancing with my Father. His hidden past. Her quest for truth. How Nazi Vienna shaped a family's identity, by Jo Sorochinsky

The Story Keeper. Weaving the Threads of Time and Memory - A Memoir, by Fred Feldman

Krisia's Silence. The Girl who was not on Schindler's List, by Ronny Hein

Defying Death on the Danube. A Holocaust Survival Story, by Debbie J. Callahan with Henry Stern

A Doorway to Heroism. A decorated German-Jewish Soldier who became an American Hero, by Rabbi W. Jack Romberg

The Shoemaker's Son. The Life of a Holocaust Resister, by Laura Beth Bakst

The Redhead of Auschwitz. A True Story, by Nechama Birnbaum

Land of Many Bridges. My Father's Story, by Bela Ruth Samuel Tenenholtz

Creating Beauty from the Abyss. The Amazing Story of Sam Herciger, Auschwitz Survivor and Artist, by Lesley Ann Richardson

On Sunny Days We Sang. A Holocaust Story of Survival and Resilience, by Jeannette Grunhaus de Gelman

Painful Joy. A Holocaust Family Memoir, by Max J. Friedman

I Give You My Heart. A True Story of Courage and Survival, by Wendy Holden

In the Time of Madmen, by Mark A. Prelas

Monsters and Miracles. Horror, Heroes and the Holocaust, by Ira Wesley Kitmacher

Flower of Vlora. Growing up Jewish in Communist Albania, by Anna Kohen

Aftermath: Coming of Age on Three Continents. A Memoir, by Annette Libeskind Berkovits

Not a real Enemy. The True Story of a Hungarian Jewish Man's Fight for Freedom, by Robert Wolf

Zaidy's War. Four Armies, Three Continents, Two Brothers. One Man's Impossible Story of Endurance, by Martin Bodek

The Glassmaker's Son. Looking for the World my Father left behind in Nazi Germany, by Peter Kupfer

The Apprentice of Buchenwald. The True Story of the Teenage Boy Who Sabotaged Hitler's War Machine, by Oren Schneider

The Cello Still Sings. A Generational Story of the Holocaust and of the Transformative Power of Music, by Janet Horvath

---

The series **Jewish Children in the Holocaust** consists of the following autobiographies of Jewish children hidden during WWII in the Netherlands:

Searching for Home. The Impact of WWII on a Hidden Child, by Joseph Gosler

See You Tonight and Promise to be a Good Boy! War memories, by Salo Muller

Sounds from Silence. Reflections of a Child Holocaust Survivor, Psychiatrist and Teacher, by Robert Krell

Sabine's Odyssey. A Hidden Child and her Dutch Rescuers, by Agnes Schipper

The Journey of a Hidden Child, by Harry Pila with Robin Black

---

The series **New Jewish Fiction** consists of the following novels, written by Jewish authors. All novels are set in the time during or after the Holocaust.

The Corset Maker. A Novel, by Annette Libeskind Berkovits

Escaping the Whale. The Holocaust is over. But is it ever over for the next generation? by Ruth Rotkowitz

When the Music Stopped. Willy Rosen's Holocaust, by Casey Hayes

Hands of Gold. One Man's Quest to Find the Silver Lining in Misfortune, by Roni Robbins

The Girl Who Counted Numbers. A Novel, by Roslyn Bernstein

There was a garden in Nuremberg. A Novel, by Navina Michal Clemerson

The Butterfly and the Axe, by Omer Bartov

Good for a Single Journey, by Helen Joyce

The series **Holocaust Books for Young Adults** consists of the following novels, based on true stories:

The Boy behind the Door. How Salomon Kool Escaped the Nazis. Inspired by a True Story, by David Tabatsky

Running for Shelter. A True Story, by Suzette Sheft

The Precious Few. An Inspirational Saga of Courage based on True Stories, by David Twain with Art Twain

Jacob's Courage: A Holocaust Love Story, by Charles S. Weinblatt

---

The series **WW2 Historical Fiction** consists of the following novels, some of which are based on true stories:

Mendelevski's Box. A Heartwarming and Heartbreaking Jewish Survivor's Story, by Roger Swindells

A Quiet Genocide. The Untold Holocaust of Disabled Children WW2 Germany, by Glenn Bryant

The Knife-Edge Path, by Patrick T. Leahy

Brave Face. The Inspiring WWII Memoir of a Dutch/German Child, by I. Caroline Crocker and Meta A. Evenly

When We Had Wings. Living in the World's First Democratic Orphanage of Janusz Korczak, by Tami Shem-Tov

Want to be an AP book reviewer?

Reviews are very important in a world dominated by the social media and social proof. Please drop us a line if you want to join the *AP review team*. We will then add you to our list of advance reviewers. No strings attached, and we promise that we will not be spamming you.

info@amsterdampublishers.com

www.ingramcontent.com/pod-product-compliance
Lightning Source LLC
LaVergne TN
LVHW041935070526
838199LV00051BA/2793